16-690

DE

STRENGTH OF WILL

First impression—December 1915
Second impression—February 1916
Third impression—May 1916
Fourth impression—August 1916
Fifth impression—November 1916

STRENGTH OF WILL

BY

E. BOYD BARRETT, S.J.

M.A. Hons. (Nat. Univ. of Ireland)
D.Ph. (Louvain Univ.)

Author of "Motive Force and Motivation Tracks"

P. J. KENEDY & SONS

44 BARCLAY STREET, NEW YORK

TO
SURGEON BOYD BARRETT

FOREWORD

IN these pages an effort is made to give a plain account of the Will, and to indicate a method whereby it may be improved and strengthened.

An effort is made also to present the matter in an attractive way, so that a certain interest may be taken in the activities of the Will, and so that, when familiarised with introspection, one may find profit and amusement from studying the details of the wonderful life that goes on within.

As far as possible technical terms and abstruse discussions are avoided. Indeed, there seems no need to introduce metaphysics, as our method is to observe and describe, as do experimentalists, and to keep close to what is concrete. These pages tell of what is felt and seen, not of course by the fingers or eyes the body, but by the faculties of the mind. The spirit can probe and poke about into its own dark corners, and can ride fast after its own swift movements. Of what it observes and learns, on such occasions, and of what it does, these pages tell.

We assume, of course, that readers are already tolerably well informed as to the nature and chief functions of the Will. Further, we suppose that they are aware of the value and worth of having a strong, effective will. Finally, we flatter ourselves that readers are not without some inclination and intention to bestir themselves in the direction of improving their own wills.

It is not with the purpose of substituting this book for other books on the Will that these pages are written, but rather of supplementing them in one important point. The books which already hold the field are excellent from many points of view, but from one point of view they are deficient. *They do not suggest a practical method of will-training.* They are written on the "Education of the Will," but they are not helpful to those who seek a definite method of strengthening and of improving the Will.

One word more in conclusion. As far as possible references to other books are avoided, but references to experiences are frequent. The reason is that *our standpoint is not that of authority, but of experiment.* The experiments referred to have been carried on, at times with the strictest scientific exactitude, as those conducted at Louvain University from 1909 to 1911; at times with less scientific rigour, as those conducted at Clongowes Wood College, Co. Kildare, Ireland, from 1913 to 1914. Even in quoting from experiments we have endeavoured to be as little tedious as possible, and have striven to awaken interest in what should be the most fascinating part of Psychology.

CONTENTS

SECTION I

GENERAL NOTIONS ABOUT WILL-TRAINING

SECTION I

GENERAL NOTIONS ABOUT WILL-TRAINING

THOSE who think of devoting themselves to body-training are not repelled by the knowledge that daily exercises, which demand a certain sacrifice of time, and a certain expenditure of effort, are called for. It seems to them quite reasonable to pay the cost of what they buy. They are purchasers of well-developed muscles and finely shaped limbs, and they pay readily in daily portions the price, which is bodily exercise. In like manner those who wish to train their memories are quite prepared to undertake certain tasks at certain times. It would be strange if it were otherwise with those who desire to train their wills.

Will-training is, of course, a gradual process, and in this it resembles body-training and memory-training. Little by little the will is built up. Little by little it is developed and perfected and frees itself from taint and disease. *It is a slow process, but a very sure process.* It demands, needless to say, much time and much earnestness.

Over and above time and earnestness, will-training costs effort, and that means self-sacrifice. Indeed, it is true to say that will-training costs what we are least ready to pay, for the discipline of daily exercises means self-sacrifice. It is better to admit this at once, and not to pretend that a strong will can be bought with a cheque, or won with a smile.

Strange to say, in order to train the will, will is needed. Will is self-trained. Will works on itself and perfects itself. If it did not preëxist in us, there would be nothing to perfect, and no source of strength wherewith to work. For the will is called on at every step in will-training. It is the will which builds up the will by willing. Perhaps, for the moment, these words are not plain and clear, but presently they will become so.

In will-training no expenditure of effort is fruitless. All is banked for some future occasion. But more than this, we begin to draw interest at once on what we bank. Our will grows stronger gradually, and day by day we derive benefit from the exercises we have already accomplished. This means very much, as the will enters into every action. Indeed, no faculty is so universal in its scope of activity as the will. From tying a boot-lace in the morning to switching off an electric lamp at night, the will enters into all we do.

The question will doubtless be asked, "Is it possible to train the will? If one is already advanced in age, is it still possible?" The answer is most decidedly in the affirmative. It is always possible to train, that is, to improve the will. No matter how weak and inefficient the will may have become, yet is it still possible to train it.

There is no doctrine held more tenaciously by sane psychologists than this doctrine of the possibility of restoring and rebuilding the will, even when things have gone very far.

Some wills, of course, seem more capable than others of reaching a high degree of perfection. Not many men could acquire the will-power to joke about death and suffering, like Sir Thomas More or St. Laurence, even when in the hands of executioners. But all men can increase the strength of their will, and can so far throw off lethargy and laziness of character as to become energetic and strenuous.

Having prefaced these observations about the need for time, and effort, and gradual development in will-training, it may be well to indicate an important distinction between "reform of character" and "increase of will-power."

Many authors regard the "education of the will" as synonymous with self-perfection, self-culture, and the reform of character. As a result, in books which profess to deal with will-training, much is said about the passions, ideals, sensuality, habits, meditation, day-dreaming, idea-force, self-conquest and such topics, but little is said of the precise means of curing will-disease and of acquiring will-force. Indeed, it would seem that the word *will* is taken in far too broad and too general a sense, and that *reform of character* is looked upon as quite the same thing as *increase of will-power*. Now this is certainly not so.

It is quite conceivable that a man should have a very strong will, and yet care very little for culture or for the observing of the moral law. And further, it is quite conceivable that a man should set himself to develop and train his will, and should succeed in so doing, without ever entertaining the idea of making himself a more noble or more ideal character.

Men train their memories without any reference to morality, and men may well train their wills without any reference to morality. Without doubt when will-strength is acquired, passion can more easily be controlled. Without doubt, too, it usually happens that virtue and true strength of will go hand in hand. But this does not gainsay the fact that virtue and will-strength are two quite different things, and that books professedly written on the "education of the will" should not be almost exclusively devoted to the consideration of good habits and self-culture.

A book on will-training should be as closely devoted to will-exercises, will-hygiene, and will-phenomena, as a book on body-training should be devoted to body-exercises, body-hygiene, and muscular phenomena.

The will, like the intellect, is now an instrument of good, and now of evil. The strong will, still improving and growing stronger, *may* become more and more an instrument of evil. It may co-exist with vicious passions, gross lack of culture, deplorable habits, and an utter contempt for the conventions of life. The will is an instrument, weak or powerful for good or evil, but only an instrument, although as our highest and noblest instrument it should be our object ever to perfect and raise it. That it is important to have a strong will no one will deny. We all admire the man of strong will—he is more truly a man than other

19

men. He has the power to master himself—
to become "lord of himself" and sole ruler of
his own forces. He knows what he can do. He
does what he sets himself to do. He wills to
do what he does, and means what he wills. He
knows his own mind, and puts his hand with
confidence to do that on which he is resolved,
neither over-impetuously nor over-indolently.
Lethargy has no hold on him, and he scorns
to give way to impulse. Energetic and strenuous without being over-active, he is consistent
and persevering. He is in earnest about his
work, in beginning it, in continuing it, and in
concluding it. He goes not a step beyond, nor
does he fall a step short, of the just limit of
his purpose. He uses his powers with ease
and with assurance. He seems, as it were, to
have possession of his own will; to be free in
his independence. He wills. His body in his
hands is like a machine which he uses to accomplish his ends. That machine is started
without a hitch, is governed and regulated as
to speed and direction most smoothly, and is
pulled up without a jerk by his will. No
engine-driver can control a locomotive as he
controls his body. He does not care, usually,
about boasting, or bullying, or flattering. He
is too strong for that. He is not over-anxious

to display his force. He knows he has power and he does not care if others know it or not. Rather, perhaps, he is aware that others do know and feel it intuitively. He does not display his will-force by clenching his fists, and grinding his teeth, and convulsively heaving his breast like the heroes of the cinema. He is content to face his daily tasks with quiet assurance, and to carry out what his will wills.

SECTION II

RELIGION AND WILL-TRAINING

SECTION II

RELIGION AND WILL-TRAINING

THE only will-training which the plain man undergoes is the will-training which the practice of religion affords. This is, of course, a very variable quantity. Nevertheless, in the case of a man who faithfully adheres to his religious duties it is not inconsiderable. It will be our duty now, as far as possible, to estimate its nature and extent.

In Catholicism, for it is the religion we contemplate, there are many factors which tell for the education and improvement of the will. There is, first of all, the earnest striving towards the *Summum Bonum*, towards God, which is the central fact of religion, and the great, supreme work of the will. There is next, the principle of asceticism, viz., that given a good intention in a moral act, the more strongly and whole-heartedly we will, the more value the act will have—for willing, as we know, can be more or less intense.[1] There is, thirdly, the discipline of regularity and fidelity in religious exercises; and, lastly, the practice of internal and external mortification, which is boldly and uncompromisingly insisted upon by the Church—"unless you do penance you shall all perish."

Two principles on which Catholic asceticism to a great extent reposes have close reference to the will.

(1) In acts of worship the most important element, the element whereby we merit, is will and intention.

(2) In attaining virtue and self-perfection, our chief aim should be to go against ourselves, that is, to utilise our will in overcoming passion.

The Catholic religion calls for great regularity in worship. There are yearly, and weekly, and daily duties. There are vigils of feasts and long periods, Lent and Advent, to be kept in the spirit of penance. There are

[1] *Vide* St. Thomas (De Malo, q. 3, a. 11 ad 3), where he refers to greater or lesser intensity of willing.

"Voluntarium dicitur cujus principium est in ipso agente. Et ideo *quanto principium interius magis augetur*, tanto etiam peccatum fit gravius."

duties, hard and severe for the human heart, to be undergone. Confession, and fasting, and weekly Mass. In all things the spirit of order prevails—even in the smallest details. How and when to use Holy Water, how and when to recite the Office—in all particulars there is perfect method. The discipline of the whole system is faultless. There is no disorder, no uncertainty. Nothing is left to chance. The will submits to rule, and in embracing religion it embraces order and regularity. It seeks to form for itself good habits, and finds therein the foundation of virtue. It finds, in fact, that in practising virtue it is learning to will well, and that in willing well it is practising virtue.

As we shall see later on, one of the best exercises for the will is to put before itself a clear, well-defined task which is not too difficult and to set itself in all earnestness to accomplish it. Now, this is precisely the kind of exercise that religion affords the will. Let the task be to attend Mass next Sunday, or to fast next Friday, or to make restitution on such a date for something stolen. In each case the duty is clear and well-defined. Seriousness and earnestness in the accomplishment of the duty, are in each case evoked by the consideration of

27

the moral gravity of neglecting it. The will has to brace itself up, to face the task bravely, and to fulfil it completely. An *effort* is called for, and that effort is good for the will.

But further than this religion improves the will by calling for *reiterated efforts*. An isolated effort is of little significance in will-education, whereas regularly repeated efforts mean very much. Now religion calls for the methodical expenditure of effort. Let us take the simple case of morning prayers. It is not enough to say them occasionally or fairly often. *We are asked to say them every morning.* That is, we are asked, every morning, to make an effort. So it is for nearly all the duties of religion. They recur. They demand reiterated efforts. The will is not suffered to lie fallow. It is kept constantly at work. No doubt, habit smoothes away the harsh shock of effort, and automatism comes to our help, but nevertheless there is always the fundamental necessity of making efforts. One of the points in which religion does most for the will is its regard to resolutions. To make and keep a good resolution is a power that every faithful Catholic has to acquire. Now *to resolve* is an act of the will. It means that the will chooses a *bonum,* an end or object, and aims at its acqui-

28

sition. It wills, seeks, strives for, and desires that *bonum* with more or less intensity.

Now, as our whole moral good frequently depends on the making and keeping of a good resolution, the Catholic Church has taught us through her ascetic writers how to do so. Further, she aids us in every way to make and keep good resolutions, thus doing an inestimable work for the education of the will.

It may perhaps be well to dwell on this point, so as to bring out clearly the part of religion in will-training.

Catholic ascetics teach us, in this matter, first of all to have a clear and definite view of the object we propose to ourselves—let us suppose that it is to overcome the passion of anger. Now the resolution "not to give way to anger" would be far too broad and too great. Applying the principle, *"divide et impera,"* we content ourselves with resolving "not to give way to external manifestations of anger." But here again, our resolution is too broad and too great. We again apply the principle, *"divide et impera,"* and resolve "not to give way to angry retorts." This resolution is pointed, definite and intelligible—it means that cross and peevish remarks must not occur. A time limit may now be added in order to make the resolution still more well-defined. "Until the last day of this month I will not make an angry retort." Possibly, it might be advisable to limit this resolution still more, by conditions of place or circumstance, adding "in such a place or to such a person, or during such a ceremony," but we shall suppose that to be unnecessary.

The resolution being now well formulated, the task of making it begins. Merely to say it over or to promise it in a feeble way is absolutely useless. The whole will, with the whole force and energy of the will, must be brought into it. Not only that, but the whole living strength of the will must be literally hurled into it, not once or twice, but again and again each day, right up to the very last day of the month.

The resolution must be meant. We must be able to say, "Yes! before God, I mean that! I mean it as intensely and really as I can ever mean anything! I will keep that resolution. I know I can and will keep it because I mean it. Further, I will take every precaution to keep it alive and vigorous within me by re-making it again and again."

Needless to say such resolutions should not be lightly made, nor should they be trifled with. In them the credit of the will is at stake. It is a serious thing to make a serious resolution, and it is a bad thing to break one, bad for the will and bad for self-respect.

Now, Catholic writers suggest many means whereby we may render our resolutions more secure.[2] We must pray for the grace to keep them. Supernatural aid will then be ours; but prayer will also aid us naturally. We must meditate on the advantages of keeping it and on the disadvantages of breaking it, on the beauty of patience and on the pettiness and shame of irritability. Our mind will be convinced by this means, and our emotions will be aroused in favour of the resolution. Next, we are advised to intensify our resolution not merely by direct will-acts, but by indirect will-acts derived from self-inflicted penance. For pain and hunger will make us more in earnest and will make our "meaning" more sincere.

Such, in general, is the method which Catholics are taught to employ in the matter of resolutions. Needless to say, if this method is faithfully employed the will grows strong and energetic—its good qualities are developed and

[2] One practical method is to make the "Particular Examen," which consists in a half-daily examination of our failures or success in our resolution.

its faults are corrected. Of course, it must not be thought that religion in itself wholly consists in making and keeping good resolutions. This is not so. Nevertheless, to a great extent, religion depends on the making and keeping of good resolutions, as on its method.

It may perhaps be well to take a type of will-hero, whose strength of will was the outcome of religion. Such a one was John Berchmans, a young Flemish Jesuit of the early seventeenth century.[3] His name is unknown to the literary and political world, but none the less he was possessed of remarkable gifts of mind. The chief note of his character was moderation and good-sense, combined with an extraordinary tenacity of purpose. If he put before himself some end to be gained, he devoted his whole strength towards achieving it, and he regarded every tiny detail involved in this pursuit of his end as of the most serious consequence—*maximi minima habuit*. He combined the qualities of miser and spendthrift in such matters, being most miserly about allowing himself the slightest deviation from his purpose or the slightest delay in winning it, whereas he was most lavish and generous in giving himself and all he had to

[3] Such another was the better-known St. Teresa.

the working out of his aim. In him the maxim was verified to the fullest: *"Suae quisque vitae pictor est; artifex hujus operis est voluntas."* He set himself to become a saint in a new way, by doing ordinary things extremely well, and thanks to his lifelong pertinacity of purpose he gained his end.

That he sought in religion strength and inspiration is of course indisputable. To fulfil perfectly all his religious duties was the main object of his life, and it was in fulfilling them that the promptness, consistency and persevering regularity of his will were manifested.

It would not be difficult to find among the annals of the Saints many other examples of will-heroes: some were men of extraordinary energy, like Francis Xavier, some of extreme gentleness, like Francis de Sales, some of cold intellectual intensity, like Ignatius, some of child-like sweetness, like Antony of Padua. In each case great will-strength followed in the wake of religious perfection. In each case converse with God raised and developed the will-faculty, just as it improved every other faculty of the mind.

We have seen at some length that the practice of religion implies will-training, but nevertheless it must be remembered that it is not the special aim of religion to train the will.[4] It does so only indirectly, and it does not always do so as perfectly and as surely as we might wish. *It seems necessary to have some specific training.* To train the will, as it were, for the sake of the will itself, for the sake of the perfection of the will, and not for the sake of other things.[5]

The will must be taught, to some extent, to will for the sake of willing. The will builds

[4] From one point of view it is the object of religion to train the will—to train it to abstain from sin and to train it to embrace God by will—love.

[5] We append a quotation from a paper read at the "International Congress of Moral Education," 1912, by Dr. J. H. Abendanon. Making allowance for his point of view, the quotation is of interest and instructive.

"On prétend souvent que la religion peut suffire à l'éducation morale, c'est-à-dire à la formation du caractère et à l'affermissement de la volonté. Il est cependant de notoriété courante que la foi religieuse n'est pas un empêchement pour commettre des actes criminels. Sans cela la statistique criminelle devrait varier d'après le degré de religiosité des differentes countrées. La religion peut coopérer d'une façon très efficace à l'éducation morale; elle en est même un des plus puissants auxiliaires, et les belles maximes qu'elle répand sont les meilleurs guides dans la vie humaine, mais seulement à condition d'aller de pair avec le relèvement et l'exercice continuel de la volonté. C'est en outre une chose reconnue par ceux qui sont à la tête des écoles confessionelles que l'éducation y présente une lacune. Eh bien, cette lacune n'est autre chose que le défaut de contrôle de la volonté. Ce défaut fait que le meilleur enseignement moral reste sans effet pratique."

up will by willing. As we shall see later, it builds up will best by willing will. The will must, as it were, turn back on itself in willing, and will will. Exercises calculated to provoke willing for the sake of willing are necessary. We must feel the pure glow of pleasure involved in willing for the sake of the will. Just as the intellect or memory must be trained, apart from the training they receive in the practice of religion, so must the will be trained apart from the training it receives in this manner.

It must not, however, be overlooked that will-training of itself, *without relation to religion and morality,* is in great part meaningless. For, as Professor Förster writes, "All our efforts are lacking in deeper meaning if they are not correlated to a great spiritual view of life as a whole. Even the most perfect development of will-power tends to degenerate into a mere athletic exercise without enduring significance."[6]

[6] "Marriage and the Sex Problem," p. 207.

SECTION III

THINGS ABOUT THE WILL

SECTION III

WE know little about the will. We are aware of its spiritual nature, and we can trace it roughly in some of its activities. We are familiar with some of the phenomena which accompany willing, but that is all. Compared with the knowledge we have of the memory, what we know of the will is as nothing. We are unable to measure it, to distinguish its various types, or to juggle with it in experimentation as in the case of the memory. It is elusive. It baffles us and escapes from observation. We make plans whereby to catch a glimpse of it in its working and our plans fail. We know we have wills and that we will. We are conscious that willing is not thinking nor imagining. Most of us know little more.

The method by which we seek to study the will is the introspective method. We look into ourselves and try to see what happens. We have a choice to make. The will decides for

one or other of the alternatives. We carefully
follow the movements of the will. The play of
motives and of impulses interests us. Hesitation perhaps takes place and we follow its
growth and development. The choice-process
proceeds, develops, is completed and the choice
is made. But although we know that the will
has made its appearance and has acted the essential rôle, we have not been able to distinguish it!

Yet, whatever of importance we do know
about the will is known through introspection.
Patience and practice and skill in introspection
eventually result in our being able to observe
the will somewhat, and to distinguish the characteristics of good willing. It is fascinating
work, that of studying the will, but it is difficult and delicate. It is not hard to affirm that
there is a *will-feeling* which is quite different
from other feelings or emotional states, but
it is not easy to analyse and distinguish the
ingredients of the will-feeling. It is easy to
see that *consent* is different from *resolution,*
but it is not so easy to point out the precise
difference, in psychological elements, between
these two acts of the will. Yet it is by introspection alone that this can be done. The mind
must watch and follow and scrutinise the vari-

ous phases of volitional activity. The mind has this power, and it is a power worthy of exercise.

Many words and phrases denote volitional activities. "To make up one's mind," to resolve, to consent, to desire, to strive, to choose, to make an effort—these infinitives point to will acts. Conation, intention, willing, inhibiting, controlling, permitting, preventing, and many such words are also used of the will. When a man of character, at some crisis of his life, *makes up his mind* to adopt a certain course, and says, "I will do so and so. I am determined to do it. It is my firm intention to do it"—he is speaking of a certain state of soul that we call *willing*. This state is radically different from all other states. It is about action. It is emotional. It concerns self and is very personal. It is a law and a line of conduct. It binds and controls. It is creative and arbitrary. It means self-determination. Self rules self. It is about the future. It is about reality. It is something almost sacred.

The will has been defined as "the faculty of inclining towards or striving after some object intellectually apprehended as good." We know that there is an active side in us—a "doing" side as well as a mere recipient or passive side. We tend outwards, we attack or carry out at one time; at another we submit, undergo and suffer. Now the former state, the "*ad*" state, is that of willing. But we must tend towards something. The something towards which we tend by nature is "the good." The intellect sees and knows something useful or perfect. Our interest is aroused. We are attracted by this something. At first a mere fancy or *a vague wish* is experienced. Then a stronger wish grows into *a desire*. With the desire a certain *tending towards* is awakened. The will is now at work. We are striving, or seeking for the good. This develops into *conation* and deliberate effort to attain the good. The striving for the good is a force—a *vis appetitiva*—it is the function of the will. It may be more or less strong. It grows or wanes. It may be deep in our nature or shallow and light. If very weak and transient it will not entail long protracted work and effort. At most it will entail an impulsive effort. Or it may entail no active effort, but may only provoke a hesitation and dilatoriness of mind. Now the art of rendering this *vis appetitiva* deep and strong and lasting is the art of strengthening the will. With the man of strong will, the *vis appetitiva* is so powerful that it overcomes all obstacles, faces all difficulties, and outlives all delays. From this it is perhaps clear that the will is "the faculty of inclining towards or striving after some object intellectually apprehended as good."

It may be well to give a concrete example. Let us suppose that a boy of fifteen accompanies his father, who is a keen mountain-climber, to Switzerland. The boy overhears his father speak of a grand climb up a difficult summit. The boy's interest is aroused. His mind pictures the pleasure and honour to be gained by climbing this mountain. The achievement appears to him a *bonum*. His mind apprehends it as such. He begins to wish to do it. The wish grows. He desires. Finally he resolves to climb the mountain. He is delayed and perhaps prevented for a time. He desires and resolves all the more. Day by day his resolution grows stronger. He strives to find a good opportunity. He makes plans. He saves up to pay for guides. He makes every possible preparation. He is most *energetic* about this and quite naturally, for his will is bent on it. Everything which is calculated to help on his plans becomes desirable,

43

becomes a *bonum*. He takes a keen pleasure in his resolution. At last an opportunity presents itself, and at once, almost without an effort, he is at work climbing. In the actual fulfilment of his resolution he finds pleasure. When he succeeds and reaches the top he experiences a deep feeling of satisfaction. "The object" intellectually apprehended as good has been won!

All his acts leading up to the attainment of his end were directed by his will. The *vis appetitiva* carried him over all obstacles, and controlled all his movements until the *bonum* was gained.

We have used the expression "to will will" more than once. A word of explanation may now be offered.

It often happens that we see before us some task or work of considerable difficulty that we are inclined to shirk. We realise that it would cost us a big effort and we feel very disinclined for such an effort. Still we are intimately aware that should we set our minds to it, we could accomplish it. *If we did resolve to achieve the task we could achieve it.* But we refrain from willing. *We refuse to set our wills to the task.*

Then, a second state of mind springs up, in

the form of a question, "Shall we set our will
to work? Shall we put our will in motion?
Shall we will to will?"

Here the will is confronted with the duty
of driving itself, of putting itself to work. If
we now answer the question affirmatively and
say, "Yes! We shall put our wills in motion,"
then we really and truly *will to will*. This act
is *par excellence* the work of the will, and the
best exercise for the will. Here the will determines itself. Here the will acts most directly and most surely along the lines of good
willing. The will wills—the will wills to will!

SECTION IV
THE AWAKENING OF THE WILL

SECTION IV

THE AWAKENING OF THE WILL

I⊤ is not an easy matter to explain precisely
what the "Awakening of the Will" means, and
yet it is something very real and very important. It is not, of course, that first dawn of
wilfulness which occurs at a certain moment
in child-life, and which ushers in manhood. It
is not a first but a second spring. It is the
sudden acquisition at a later period of life
of *the sense of willing.* It comes to some but
not to all, and it is fully intelligible to none,
save to those to whom it comes.

The "Awakening of the Will" resembles to
some extent the dawn of the æsthetic sense.
All men have, beyond doubt, a native sense of
art. In few, however, is this sense wooed into
actuality and developed. Very few ever become true æsthetes, but these few find themselves at some time of their lives, and suddenly, in possession of the "sense." It bursts
open within their souls without much warning,

like a blossom. Thereafter, they taste, and feel and understand. Around them, and at their elbows throng the many, who never have tasted, and never will taste or feel or understand.

The sense of willing is however in many ways different from the æsthetic sense. It is in the first place a consciousness of a power to do rather than of a power to enjoy. It is accompanied by a feeling of achieving, rather than by a feeling of appreciating. It is a sense-thrill, springing from a knowledge of one's power to act and to control. It is not a keen delight in received impressions of symmetry, variety and beauty. It is rather the recognition of one's self in possession of one's own self-force.

The phenomenon most closely connected with the sense of willing, is the will-feeling which has already been referred to. Will-feeling accompanies every true will-act. When we make determined efforts to achieve a certain task, and when, so to speak, we are conscious of the steady heaving of the will in its straight, single purpose, we shall always find the will-feeling present. As we grow accustomed to making will-efforts, and to guiding in this or that direction the force of our will, we become aware of a certain atmosphere of willing. It is unlike the atmosphere of thinking or imagining. It is an atmosphere which seems to be pregnant with energy, activity and control. It braces and tones one up. We feel more virile and more self-confident for having been in it. It is the mental state of a brave soldier resolutely and undauntedly charging the enemy, or of an intrepid discoverer facing onwards towards his goal—as did Columbus or Captain Scott.

When the will-feeling grows habitual, and when we live more and more in the atmosphere of willing which we have described, the coming of the will-sense, or the "Awakening of the Will," is at hand. The improved condition of the will seems to react on the whole body. We grow more alert, more strenuous and more energetic. Courage and power to achieve seem to be more firmly established within. The pleasure we experience in exercising our will grows. We delight in making efforts. To control our actions has now a strange fascination for us. To accomplish a difficult task by sheer will-force now causes us a thrill of manly satisfaction. We feel ourselves more and more in possession of will-force, and at last, sooner or later, the "sense of willing" dawns upon us—and we experience the "Awakening of the Will."

It is hard to put in words or even to lead people to suspect by mere description what this sudden grasping of the reality of the will means. It is intensely reassuring and vivifying to know and grasp the fact of the will willing within us. It resembles the joy we feel at suddenly coming to know that one has done something great, or has inherited some valuable possession. The treasure hidden within has been discovered by us, and we know that nobody can steal it, and that it is in our power to use it profitably.

We have said that few men *use their will*. By that we mean that few men act as if realising the powers and limitations of their will and the best manner of putting it to work. They use their will as a Dervish would use a baseball bat or a Malay would use a pair of skates. They misuse their will and break and wreck it. They handle the most perfect and delicate of all instruments with the crude roughness of ignorance. Or else they allow their will to lie dormant, "to rust unburnished, not to shine in use." They live the lives of animals and their will is never awakened. And yet this "Awakening of the Will" is the very first task to which they should set themselves. They should call into life and activity this all-powerful force, if they have any ideal in life or any high ambition.

The "Awakening of the Will" must, however, come from within. It cannot come from without. No external treatment or influence can awaken a man's will. He must do it himself, and for himself. His will by willing must stir itself to life. It must be self-awakened, and it must keep itself awake by constant exercise. Such exercise will win health and vigour for the will.

Sometimes in a will-contest when things are going rather doubtfully and when we are in fear of giving in, a light suddenly breaks on us, and a new strength vibrates through us. We realise suddenly that we have a will and that it is there at work. "The will is there and the will can do it." The unknown mysterious something is at work and we confide in it. We feel and know that it is there and we pin our hopes to it. We have of a sudden become aware of the power and force of the will. Beyond question it is there. Beyond question it can achieve the task. Beyond question it is at work.

The "Awakening of the Will" means something very real. It marks the beginning of a new reign—the reign of the will. Spiritual vigour, will-force, energy and self-control characterise the new epoch. The will, always arbitrary and tyrannical, now rules with absolute sway. The sense of willing pervades one's life and its course is guided by purpose. We are no longer like withered leaves "carried hither and thither by every wind that blows." We guide through our will our destiny. We purpose and we achieve.

The "Awakening of the Will" is the outcome of long-continued effort. It is not won in a moment. It costs much. It means that a most powerful instrument for good or for evil is placed in our hands. Henceforth there will be more intensity and earnestness in all that we do. Our resolutions will be deep and strong and somewhat terrible in their sincerity.

To live the life of the will means that we shall gradually fall away from weaker men. Antipathy will gradually spring up between them and us. Their ways are not our ways, nor are our ways theirs. Our lives will become more solitary and more independent. In spite of ourselves we shall grow somewhat cold and serious and rigid. Some of the flower and bloom of our natural manner will be lost and

54

we shall be less lovable. Those who admire us from afar will talk vaguely of telepathy, psychic influence and magnetism, and use many meaningless terms. But they will little understand the secret of the change, and the cause of our power, for they will not know what the "Awakening of the Will" means.

To summarise the foregoing explanation of the "Awakening of the Will," it means three things:

(1) Consciousness of a new power.
(2) Acquisition of a new habit.
(3) Development of new resources.

It means, firstly, that we come to recognise ourselves as "forces" capable of achieving and controlling. It means, secondly, that we are now in a position to use our force, habitually directing and employing it with confidence and ease. It means, thirdly, that we come into possession of a mine, from which, if we work and develop it aright, we can draw untold riches.

SECTION V

THREE INTROSPECTIONS OF WILL-CONTESTS

SECTION V

For a few moments I am hesitating before beginning to write this chapter. It seems to me that it will be a very difficult matter to give good examples of introspections of will-contests. On the other hand, I cannot help thinking that it would be instructive and useful to my readers should I be able to do so, for they would then have a better understanding of my point of view with regard to the Will.

.   .   .   .

Since I have written the word Will (the last word of the last sentence) I have *resolved* to write this chapter.

First Introspection

When I say "resolved" I am doubtful if that is the right word to use, for my mind is not yet firmly made up about this matter. I

[1] This chapter is given, almost *verbatim*, as originally written.

foresee that I may be quite unable to give good examples of introspections, and it may seem to me eventually more prudent to omit this chapter. However, my mind is quite made up on the point of *attempting*. I am going most certainly to try.

Now what exactly do I find at present in my mind with regard to this resolve? I feel an ennui and a disinclination to take much trouble, but I feel also a real interest in the work. I seem to have something before me which I am to reach or acquire. There is something which I am now to get at and attain. That *want* causes a certain irritation or unsettledness of mind. I am striving and not quite at my ease. *The certain fixed resolve to try is a cause of satisfaction to me.* So much is definite, settled, satisfactory. On the other hand, the vagueness and hesitation about whether I shall write the whole chapter or not is a cause of uneasiness and distress. That hesitation is distressing, discouraging, and debilitating—I feel all that. The certainty of the minor resolution is on the other hand both encouraging and gratifying.

.   .   .   .

I paused for a moment when I arrived thus far and found it hard to restart. It is a vague

and indefinite task in which I am engaged and
so I want to be out of it as soon as possible.
It seems to lead, not exactly nowhere, but to
no place of importance.

. . . .

The knowledge that I am trying brings with
it a feeling of satisfaction. Then I am conscious that my will is guiding me and urging
me on. I must obey it. It is ruling me. It
seems unnecessarily serious and earnest about
so trivial a thing. It seems somehow dragging
me after it and I must follow—and indeed it
seems something apart from me and yet having
complete control over me.

There are many things in my mind at present that I should like to describe, but it would
take too long. Of course there are many feelings of pressure, fatigue, hurry, strain, tension and other such-like. They do not matter,
and it is on the will-phenomena that I must
concentrate my attention. The feeling of yearning, or want, or desire to achieve, is still there.
Then the feeling of purpose—the will-feeling
that I am acting under orders from the will is
there, but obscurely. Now I seem to be writing
more or less automatically. It does not cause
much trouble and is not fatiguing. But back
again to the Will!

61

I must make a fair attempt. A something, a duty to be fulfilled is before me, and I feel a sure confidence that I shall not fail in my duty. Indeed, just now I am beginning to be conscious that I have fulfilled it already! There is a certain *throbbing* as it were, or rhythmic movement in my will-acts—keeping me still to the task. This throbbing is gentle and not unpleasant. It marks a series of quiet, semi-conscious efforts. From time to time as I go along my lips form the words, "I will do it. I will carry out my task." I know from old experience of such tasks that I shall not be in fault. A sense of power and strength is also present. But this will-task is so easy and even agreeable; and there is so little opposition provoked that the sense of power seems out of place. There has been no sharp contest, no hard-won victory.

As I write now, and feel that what I have written may be of use, an intention of finishing this chapter is gradually taking shape. It may not be so hard, after all. A certain desire to do it well is awakening in me. It would not now cost the will very much to make the resolution of finishing the chapter.

The background, for there is one, to all the phenomena I have mentioned is a dull, massive

kind of emotion, not painful, not cognitive, but
apparently urging on to action or at least connected with action. It may be best described
as conative. Of the will all I can say is that I
know it is at work—I may say, constantly at
work—I cannot of course see it in image as I
should see a memory picture, but still I am intimately conscious that it is at work. It seems
to move as it were in its own sphere, colourless,
soundless, and tasteless, but real, active, and
vital. *It does not seem anywhere—but still it
is present.* It seems to go in a direction, out-
ward and onward, towards its object, which
seems ahead! So much and no more can I say
of it.

Second Introspection

Let us suppose that we find ourselves stand-
ing, on a rather cold evening, at the end of a
spring-board, prepared for a plunge. We have
come down to bathe, thinking it would be nice
and warm, and now it has turned rather chilly.
Something has to be done, we cannot return
without bathing, and yet the water looks cold
and uninviting. We cross our arms, rub our
shins together, shiver a little, wish we were
anywhere else, and *hesitate*.

The task of plunging seems harder and

harder, the longer we hesitate. We know that, and resolve to go in before very long—but that very long is indefinite. The thought of the coldness of the water, and of the nasty shock of the first contact, holds us back. A certain *inertia* takes possession of us and we find it hard to take action. We feel the board under our feet, and the wind which tosses our hair. We see and hear things very distinctly and yet we take little interest in what we see or hear. At the focus of consciousness is the thought—"I must after all go in." We know that if we brace up our wills to the task—*if we will to will*—that we shall be able to plunge in; *but we refuse to will to will*—we don't want to put that constraint on ourselves. It seems too cruel.

Meanwhile things are getting worse and coming to a climax. We feel colder. The task seems harder. But the necessity of action is more and more stringent. We are gradually, although unconsciously, and seemingly against our will, being moved forward. We are tending closer and closer towards the climax. Little now separates us from our fate. The will is no longer affected very much by motives for or against. Force of habit now decides all. For a moment our eyes rest on the water, the image of ourselves swimming about grows more and more realistic. A momentary "blankness" seems to pass across the surface of consciousness. We become aware that an effort has just been made—and that our toes are kicking away from the board—we are now plunging into the water and the will-act is over.

The *critical point* was reached just before we plunged. It was reached partly owing to the force of motives and partly owing to the habits of the will. The will was forced to act by the fatalism of the situation. *Something had to be done*. One cannot stand for long on the end of a spring-board. The precise moment of the plunge was determined by many factors and conditions. Some of these conditions are revealed in consciousness but many lie hidden. The act was not a good will-act. The element of hesitation and chance entered in and spoiled it. The will did not pronounce a definite *hic et nunc!* It allowed itself to be carried forward by things other than itself. In consequence, the resulting feeling was not one of satisfaction nor of moral grandeur. Indeed, it was rather one faintly tinged with shame, and faintly tinged with a certain disappointment. A sense of failure was there.

Third Introspection

The resolution I made was absolutely rigid. I would not go into the sitting-room all day. I was perfectly resolved on that. I simply *would not go in!* Then the thought came to me, but if, for instance, I heard some one calling for help in there. If some one was dying in it, would I go in? Then I saw that my resolution was *conditioned*. "I simply would not go in *unless* something extraordinary happened."

My resolve was then definite, clear, practical. In a way it was *absolute*. Under ordinary circumstances I would on no account go into the sitting-room that day!

But what, if towards evening I were to forget my resolution and go in? Then, I set myself to obviate such a mischance by renewing and repeating my resolution and reminding myself of it again and again. I sat down and thought it out. I wrote it across the surface of my mind many times. I made will-acts and will-efforts about it. My resolution grew deeper and stronger and more earnest. I shuddered to think that I should break it. I should have felt myself discredited and dishonoured. I walked quietly over and put my hand on the

66

handle of the door, and then drew it back as if with horror. *"No! never! I must not go into the sitting-room to-day."*

I felt that my resolution was unnatural, almost hysterical. But I did not care. My interest lay in rendering it stronger and in guarding it intact.

As a point of honour I felt it incumbent on me to take every step to prevent the breaking of my resolution. Besides reminding myself of it, and renewing and reënforcing it by will-acts, I decided to avoid all occasions of breaking it. Perhaps some visitors might come in the afternoon, and it might be my duty to show them into the sitting-room. I made up my mind to go out for a bicycle-ride, so as not to meet them. As I was going towards my bicycle I had to pass by the sitting-room. Suddenly I heard a voice calling from within, "Jack, is that you?" I hesitated a moment—then without answering ran on, got my bike, and rode away.

In the evening I was asked to come and play cards in the sitting-room, but I said, rather awkwardly, I think, "No, I've got a headache and I'll go to bed early."

All I cared about now was to hold out for a few hours more, till midnight, so as not to violate my promise. It had, of course, become an obsession for me. The thought was in my mind nearly all day. I was worried about it, but felt at the same time a real thrill of pride in my fidelity. I felt that, in this at least, I was a man of iron will. For $1000 I would not have broken that promise. Of course, I hoped, and was sure, that no one would offer me $1000 to go into the sitting-room. But still, strange to say, there seemed to my feverish mind some slight possibility of such a thing happening!

At last night came and I slept. I had held out manfully. The task was, of course, excessively easy and trivial, but the amount of will-force that I put into observing it was very considerable! *I had indeed increased enormously the difficulty of the task by calling up such enormous efforts to fulfil it.*

The effect of this experiment on my character was considerable. It gave me a taste of the splendid courage required to make an iron resolution. It gave me a great respect for such resolutions, and the moral pride and satisfaction which I experienced showed me very clearly that resolutions bring their own rewards.

. . . .

From the three introspections which I have given, readers will be able to judge what the nature of will-phenomena is. They will understand too the necessity of exercising themselves in introspecting and of carefully analysing their own will efforts.

SECTION VI

THE WILL AND THE INTELLECT

SECTION VI

THE effect of the will on the intellect is worthy of deep study. There is, of course, a certain antagonism between the will and the intellect, as there is between the will and physical strength. The will can be perfectly calm and at ease while muscles are straining and limbs racked with pain. So, too, the will can be calm and at ease while the intellect is feverishly ranging in the fields of thought. The will goads and drives on the intellect, just as it goads and drives on the body. There is no doubt that it accounts for mental vigour and that it improves the intellect by making it take plenty of exercise. It forces it to be sharp and thorough. It forces it also to concentrate, now on this object and now on that. It taxes its strength, but at the same time it calls up and infuses energy into its activities. The will when working awakens, as we have seen, a certain atmosphere of mind, of which we are keenly aware, and which tends for the moment to dim our consciousness of other mental phenomena. Still, this will-atmosphere is so healthful and bracing that it reacts beneficially on the intellect. Indeed it does not seem too much to say that the more and better we will, the more and better we shall think. For the toning up of the will seems somehow or other, and the reason is not very clear, to tone up and brace up the intellect as well.

Knowing and willing are, of course, man's highest and chief functions. They are the *light* and *force* of life. Intellect shows the way, and will supplies the driving power. Without intellect, will would be a blind impulse, dark and dangerous as a cyclone in the night. Without will, intellect would be a brilliant but a vain flash. It would be pretty, of course, as the wan glimmer of a light-house set in a sun-down blaze, but quite as useless.

The chief service that the intellect renders to the will is to study and take mental possession of the end or *bonum*. It sees the value of this object, and weighs its relations, merits and deficiencies. It holds it in image before the emotions that love or aversion may be aroused. It obeys the will inasmuch as it examines the favourable or unfavourable points in the *bonum* and supplies positive and negative motives for the process of deliberation, which precedes the final choice of the will.

The services that the will renders to the intellect are perhaps less direct. The will, while utilising the intellect as a kind of searchlight to be turned hither and thither, improves it by this very exercise. It makes it keener, and more capable of prolonged attention. It may, of course, injure it by overwork, or it may allow it to lie fallow too long, but on the whole its influence is for good. The pressure of the will tells for a higher and more strenuous intellectual life, and as we have pointed out the toning up of the will means the toning up and bracing up of the intellect as well.

An important difference between the will and the intellect lies in the fact that the former is *interested*, while the latter is utterly *disinterested* in all its actions. The intellect has no ulterior purpose in knowing. It learns because it sees, but not in order to see. No doubt, it learns more and more, the better it is in quality, and the longer its period of application. But it does not acquire knowledge for use or for pleasure—"it only *sees* because it must."

On the other hand, the will always wills to

gain some end. It is avariciously interested.[1]
It does not move, save to acquire something.
It stirs only to get nearer to its end, its *bonum*.
It makes the intellect, and the memory and all
the other faculties coöperate in its own interested career. It rules like a tyrant, with absolute and selfish sway. It imposes its orders
on all the little functionaries of the state of
man. It is utterly utilitarian, and in no way
artistic. It is not beauty, but force.

The intellect in face of the will is, in a
sense, a slave. It must obey. It must go
whither the will points out. But still it is
a truthful, and, in a way, an independent slave.
If commanded to do so, it will set itself to
study mathematics, but will never be forced
into believing that the three angles of a tri-
angle are unequal to two right angles, nor will
it ever be coerced into rejecting the conclusion
of a logical syllogism of which it admits the

[1] St. Teresa, who was a profound psychologist, compares the
firm, patient will to the prudent bee which remains in the hive
in order to extract honey from the flowers which its companions bring it. "For if, instead of staying in the hive, all the
bees went out one after the other, how could the honey be
made?" Elsewhere she refers to the relations between intellect and will in ecstasies. "The understanding stays its dis-
cursive operations, but the will remains fixed in God by love;
it rules as a sovereign." (*Vide*, "The Psychology of the
Saints," by H. Joly, pp. 113, 90.)

major and minor premises. It is an upright and conscientious slave that can never be lashed into denying evident truths. In this respect it is independent of the will, and defies its master's power.

While intellect and will are, by nature, utterly different and radically distinct functions, it is remarkable how closely connected they are when we consider a concrete act of willing. Professor James well said, "We reach the heart of our enquiry into volition when we ask by what process it is that the thought of any object comes to prevail stably in the mind." Indeed, it is a fact of common observation that in choosing, it is the alternative which somehow attracts and holds attention, that usually wins. It is better known and better understood, and this very familiarity tells largely in its favour when the moment for the act of choice arrives. It more fully possesses the intellect, and is more fully possessed by it. It prevails in the mind. "It is clearly and definitely known." What is called volitional attention is focused on it. It holds that attention. The other alternative seems strange, unfamiliar, and out in the cold. The latter has the worse position. It is in an unfavourable light. It comes to be judged harshly and perhaps unfairly—and is, in such cases, often rejected.

Now, the answer to Professor James's query, "By what process is it that such an object has prevailed stably in the mind?" is to be found in analysing *intellectual interest*. This interest reposes, no doubt, on a basis of mental habits, and has for its correlative some subtle, obscure attractiveness in the alternative itself. Be that as it may, the fact of the importance of this intellectual interest in the process of choosing, shows clearly how closely connected will and intellect are in volitional acts.

To refer briefly to experimental researches in will psychology made by the present writer, it seems that in choosing, much depends on the "clearness and definiteness" of the knowledge which one has of the alternatives. "The central fact of the researches we have been describing is that when a choice has to be made between two alternatives, the choice is quick and easy in proportion as the values of the alternatives are clearly and definitely known." [2] To continue the quotation: "In this last phrase lies, as it seems to us, the practical

[2] "Motive Force and Motivation Tracks," Longmans, 1911, p. 215.

solution of the whole problem of how to acquire a power of good motivation—and ultimately of how to choose well. We must clearly and definitely determine the values of alternatives, and that, of course, as far as possible, long before the choice begins. We must have our fixed scale of values. We must have a scale of values for every sphere in which we live, and for our life as a whole. There must be a top-value, a *ne plus ultra,* with which nothing whatever is comparable. That top-value must act as a charm, it must electrify us, hypnotise us. It must be a top-value in all reality.

"Then again there must be a lowest, a bottom-value; something which must never be chosen; something which must be rejected on every occasion as absolutely loathsome.

"There will be also middle-values and perhaps neutral values. Into such details it is not necessary to enter. The main fact, the central fact must always be kept in mind, that *the scale must be clearly and definitely known;* in consequence it must be fixed and rigidly partitioned off, each grade from that above and from that below."[3]

The will is therefore in a certain sense the handmaid of her slave. She leads and com-

[3] op. cit., p. 216.

mands the intellect, but she is strongly inclined to obey the dictates of the latter. Nay more, even when the intellect does not speak with a sure or clear voice, the will is inclined to follow in the track of mere intellectual interest. That is to say, given two alternatives of equal positive value, the one which seems *the more familiar,* even though it be in no way greater in value, is usually the one chosen. Often too it happens that the intellect points out the way to the will in so imperious a manner, that it seems as if it were, so to speak, taking the will by the arm and pushing her along in that direction.

M. Payot [4] points out very well how weak "ideas" are, *of themselves,* in provoking action. He admits, of course, their indirect force, inasmuch as they awaken the passions, which in turn strive to coerce the will. But, of themselves, and unbacked by emotion, they are but thin and lifeless shadows. His underlying thought is that the consideration of what is abstract in contradistinction to the consideration of the concrete, accompanying feelings, has little effect on the will. "Truthfulness" as a mere "idea," without vivid imagery and

[4] "L'Éducation de la Volonté," Alcan, Paris.

awakened impulses, is useless to save a boy from giving way to an advantageous falsehood. If, however, the idea awakens a sense of shame or a lively desire to be honourable, then the boy will avoid the lie.

M. Payot lays great stress on the necessity of meditation and reflection with a view to will-training. Recognising the close ties between intellect and will, he emphasises the importance of making the work of the will easier, by a cordial coöperation on the part of the intellect. Further, he shows the need of enlisting the forces of emotion and passion on behalf of the will, so that man as a whole may work for his own self-perfection.

There are, of course, many speculative questions with regard to the relations existing between the will and the intellect. Into these, however, it is by no means necessary to enter. It suffices to have shown how important it is, in view of will-training, that will and intellect should work in harmony, for their mutual advantage, and for their mutual perfection.

SECTION VII
THE SICK WILL

SECTION VII

THE SICK WILL

THE more common method of classifying maladies of the will is that of Professor James, which is easily understood. Starting from the fact that in each will there is an impulse to act, and a power to restrain action, which he calls inhibition, he divides will-maladies into two grand classes. In the first he places those wills in which the tendency to act is excessive. In the second he places those in which inhibitory power is abnormally great.

The first class is that of impulsive and impetuous wills. The second is that of phlegmatic and lethargic wills. The former are over-active, the latter are under-active. The former class are the dare-devils, the firebrands, the passionate, choleric men who throw to the winds all counsels of prudence. The latter class are the over-cautious, the listless and indolent, the sluggards and "logs," whom no exhortation can provoke to action.

85

Basing ourselves for the moment on this division we find many extraordinary examples, referred to by M. Ribot, M. Janet and other psychologists. In some cases of abnormal lethargy, or powerlessness to will (*abuleia*), men have been known to live for years like absolute logs incapable of effort. Some have, in spite of every encouragement, although their bodily organs seemed perfectly sound, been incapable of plucking up courage to raise a glass of water to their lips, or to step across the threshold of their own doors. Some men are utterly unable to resist the impulse of some idea-force—it may be that of washing their hands, or brushing their clothes, or of striving to kill some near and dear relation. The inhibitory power of the will seems to disappear totally. Cases of utter powerlessness to resist the solicitation of passion are frequent. Drunkards have faced death in order to obtain a drink, and have even mutilated their own bodies in order to excite pity and so obtain the satisfaction of their desire by getting a glass of brandy. Under hypnotic influence, many subjects are found so bereft of will-power that they act as mere tools in the hands of their hypnotisers.

It is not, however, with such extreme types

of will-disease that we are here concerned, but rather with the minor types which are met with every day. Indeed, few among us are wholly free from will-disease of some kind or other. Almost all of us are either too impetuous, or too indecisive, or hyper-active, or hyper-emotional, or in some lesser degree incapable of willing well.

The words which, in familiar conversation, we apply to people we know, show that will-maladies are not uncommon. We freely use about others such words as "listless," "indolent," "fire-brand," "sentimental," "unready," "phlegmatic," "hesitating," "hotheaded," "inert," "fussy." We say of one man that "he can never make up his mind," and of another that "the moment he gets an idea into his head he's off to do it." In each case we refer directly to some will-malady or other. Some men we find to be bullies towards inferiors, and cowards before those in authority, and we know that there is something wrong with their will. We know cases of men—minor examples of Napoleon or Parnell—who are in some respects giants of will-strength and in other respects mere pawns of passion. We are conscious too of certain men whose quiet consistency of conduct, and whose patient, perse-

vering efforts in their life's-work, stamp them
as men of healthy and strong will.

Among the more ordinary will-maladies,
which are, at the same time, particularly detrimental, we find "hesitation" and "impulsiveness." Of these we shall treat at some length.
We shall then touch briefly on some other types
which are also of consequence.

(1) *Hesitation*

Hesitation may occur before any will-act,
and may vary in intensity, duration, and even
in quality. At times it is accompanied by painful oscillations to and fro between alternatives.
At times it is an acute state of suspense and
helplessness. The mind seeming to hang in a
kind of agony between two decisions—per-
plexed and bewildered and utterly at a loss
what to do. Weariness, dejection, and discouragement are experienced, and a longing takes
possession of the soul to get out of the hesitation anyhow, somehow. As a result, the choice
or decision which is made, is usually a poor,
slipshod one. Some extrinsic, unimportant motive prevails, and the will acts in pique or despair. Regret and disappointment are felt
afterwards, and the mind feels fagged and

wearied. The choices so made are usually irresponsible and inconsistent—this, indeed, is the chief evil of hesitation.

"It destroys all possibility of acting on strictly reasonable grounds, of deciding for intrinsic motives. Subjects in hesitation seize on the first motive which comes to mind, no matter how unimportant. To save themselves the pain of further deliberation they choose recklessly: 'I couldn't arrive at a decision. Then I preferred B without really knowing the reason'; 'I chose X to escape the hesitation, without having any conscious motive for X.' Such motivations, in which purely extrinsic motives win, naturally lead to habits of random choosing." [1]

Now, what are the conditions of hesitation? Strange to say, hesitation is in great part a habit. It grows on one, not so much on account of any defect in one's will, as on account of having often hesitated before. It is, in part, a nervous malady, and the laws of association have much to say to nervousness. If we hesitate once in a certain circumstance, we are likely to hesitate again in similar circumstances.

"Prescinding from the personal character of

[1] "A Research in Will Psychology," p. 177. By E. Boyd Barrett. Longmans, 1911.

the subjects, we found that, if having made a choice they allowed themselves to repine over it, or to be annoyed for having made it; or if they made a choice in a haphazard, irresponsible manner, that is, without careful motivation, or if they chose without clear knowledge of the relative values of the alternatives, they were extremely likely to hesitate when the same choice occurred again. Indeed, careless and superficial valuations, and futile repinings over past choices, seem to predispose strongly towards future hesitations.''[2]

A more general condition of hesitation, however, is to be found.

''Hesitations occur much more frequently in disagreeable choices, and seem in a certain sense to be conditioned by them, just as they, in a certain sense, seem to condition inconsistencies. Indeed the unpleasant experience of choosing between two disagreeable substances tended to inhibit volitional functioning —and to justify the theory formulated by Mr. Stout: 'In principle it seems a safe generalisation that agreeable experience is favourable, and disagreeable experience is unfavourable, to the effective discharge of mental functions.' ''[3]

[2] op. cit., p. 173.
[3] op. cit., p. 175.

Hesitation is, then, a veritable disease of the will. It grows and spreads, exhausting the strength of the will and causing it to deteriorate. It is found both in phlegmatic and impulsive characters, but is naturally most common in the former. It besets the will, especially when the latter is fatigued and debilitated—whereas it is less potent for evil when body and will are in vigorous health.

(2) *Impulsiveness*

Impulse is one of the most interesting and one of the strangest features of the will. It is at the same time a valuable asset and a dangerous possession. In very many cases—usually, we may say—it leads to harm. On the other hand, without *impulse* we could do nothing great or difficult. It does most harm in persons of a hedonic (pleasure-seeking) temperament. Such persons are often quite resolved to follow a certain course of action, when a sudden psychic movement in another direction occurs, and all their plans are upset. Nothing is more frequent than the occurrence of impulsive choices, due to hidden, strong, conative tendencies, which are hard to analyse. They occur at various phases of the choice process, sometimes at the beginning, and sometimes at the end. The sudden force of a new hedonic attraction suffices at times to make us change our choices quite automatically. Our hand seems to turn from that to which it is tending, and to take something else. To quote an example. . . . "I saw Z at the left and understood it immediately as good, and without delay I wished to take it. In the meantime I was making a movement well directed towards Z. I had reacted, but at that moment I saw K. *My hand turned* as I saw and understood that K was better, and I took K. The direction of my hand formed a curve. At what stage of the phenomenon I was when I saw and understood K I don't know. I was quite near Z. My hand at the last instant took K. I was content in taking K; it was much better than Z."

Just as we experience sudden attractions and impulses towards an object, we experience sudden repulsions and impulses from objects. Spontaneous dynamic movements occur, an output of ill-directed force. We go towards or away from something with speed and with strength. Our reserve store of energy is called upon, and the wind fills our sails, and we are off, whither we know not. Carried away, impelled, attracted, drawn, magnetised, coerced by hidden power—whatever be the best word to describe psychic impulse—the fact is undoubted.

"In hysterics, epileptics, and criminals of the neurotic class, called *dégénérés* by French authors, there is," writes Professor James,[4] "such a native feebleness in the mental machinery, that before the inhibitory ideas can arise, the impulsive ones have already discharged into act. In persons healthy-willed by nature, bad habits can bring about this condition, especially in relation to particular sorts of impulse."

Impulsiveness often causes a sudden collapse of will. Unexpectedly all gives way and we fall to the ground in a heap. It is not so much that our will is running away with us, as that our will has run away and left us. Inhibitory power is absolutely wanting. This happens most frequently in people of a high-strung nature. "The hysterical temperament," writes Professor James,[5] "is the playground *par excellence* of this unstable equilibrium. One of these subjects will be filled with what seems the most genuine and settled aversion to a certain line of conduct, and the very

[4] "Text-book of Psychology," p. 438.
[5] op. cit., p. 438.

93

next instant follows the stirring of temptation and plunges in it up to the neck.''

(3) *Inactive Wills*

Many people seem to glide along without ever taking a strenuous part in life's battle. They go whither inclination or passion leads them. They never become masters of their own destinies, nor do they ever control their actions in a purposeful way. They carry out no resolution, pursue no end, make no sacrifice. The life of the will is unknown to them. They drive no plough across the fields of life. They ''droop and drowse,'' inert, and indifferent, listless and will-less. Their existence is a burden to them, for they have created no interest. Debilitated and aimless, they are unable to stimulate themselves. All is lethargy, weariness and depression, all is weight without strength.

For such men, the one hope is to awaken the will, and to stir it to life. This can be done in one way alone and it can only be done gradually. A beginning must be made by effort. A small effort at first, and that repeated daily. Then a greater effort and so on.

For such men, the exercises which we shall suggest will afford hope.

(4) *"I simply can't will"*

We meet men who are dispirited, and discouraged, who tell us that they can't make any more efforts. They have tried so often and failed, that they have no longer any hope. They are not like the men of inactive wills, of whom we have just treated. They are superior to them in every way, for they have made efforts. But now further effort seems useless, and impossible.

This state of mind, "I simply can't will," is due in part to ill-health and debilitation, but in still greater part it is due to an excessive ignorance of psychology. "Of course, you can still will. Of course, you can still make efforts, and you will be able to do so to the last hour of your life. But you are trying to do things beyond your strength. You can't make those efforts because they are too great. That is why you have failed.

"But make *small* efforts which are well within your strength. Make them daily, and make them regularly. Build up the health of your will once more. Reawaken the life of your will.

95

Strengthen yourself, patiently, by well regulated exercises, and then you will be well able for the big efforts which at present you find too great."

(5) *Over-active Wills*

Some men seem to "spread themselves out" too much. They diffuse their energies in every direction, and speed madly in the wake of every fresh idea. They exercise no discrimination. They retain no supply of energy for important duties. They are over-active, excitable, hot-brained, fussy, and unpractical. They waste and misuse their will-force. All their strength seems to burn itself out in a sudden, useless blaze, and they remain limp and impotent.

This type of malady is, of course, allied to "impulsiveness." It is common and so serious that it renders men otherwise gifted, useless and harmful. It springs from restlessness of mind, an eagerness and uneasiness to be doing something, to be active. We can't keep still, or hold ourselves in, or rest idle. We must expend energy. Our minds experience a whirl of ideas and plans. We want to do this and that, to go hither and thither, to seek here and there. We are soaked in impulsiveness, and the spirit of striving. We are tending, attracted, drawn or repelled in a hundred ways.

For this type of malady the only cure seems to be to acquire a habit of concentrated action. To practise oneself in making a resolution and devoting oneself wholly, with all one's strength, to the carrying out of that resolution and none other. In this way *a habit of focusing will-force will be gradually won.*

(6) *Emotional Wills*

Some men are predominantly emotional and sentimental in character. Their souls are full of sensible impulses and movements. They live by feeling rather than by thought or action. They are steeped and soaked in emotion and there is no output of action. The will is so swathed and wrapped around and closely hugged by feelings and yearnings and sentimental impulses that it is unable to break through and act. Such men find it hard to realise that there is an *infinite* difference between will and feeling. Their only achievements take place in dreamland. The will's energy, such as it is, is spent in imaginary activity. No lotus nor opiate could produce so dulling an effect as the breath of this deep sentimentality.

It drugs the soul as opium never drugged it.

For such men the obvious necessity is to secure that a certain amount of deliberate, purposeful activity should enter into their lives. This activity, at first, may well take the form of will-tasks such as we shall presently suggest. By means of them, they will gradually obtain control and possession of their own wills, and will be enabled to utilise them with effect in the various circumstances of their lives.

(7) *The Over-practical Will*

There is a type of will directly opposed to that which we have just been considering, which we shall call, for want of a better name, the over-practical will. This kind of will is found frequently in active, busy men who are wholly immersed in their daily plans and schemes and duties. Such men lose the sense of proportion, and while they carry out with admirable determination the tiny purposes of their daily lives, they seem almost wholly bereft of lofty ideals and high aims. They are taken up entirely with the *hic et nunc*. They never look far ahead. They never try to synthetise their various aims into one grand purpose. They are essentially "small" men.

They have brought to perfection the quality of practical effectiveness in their will, but they have failed to find a scope for the larger and broader will-impulse which consists in striving after the *Summum Bonum*, the Supreme Good.

They reduce the will to a kind of penny-in-the-slot machine. It works admirably and returns at once a little made-up parcel when called on to do so. But it languishes and fails, all the time, for want of something greater and higher to fight for and to aim at.

(8) *The Indefinitive Will*

Many people seem strangely unconscious as to whether or not a will-act has taken place within them. They seem not to know whether or not they have really made a choice or a decision. They are unaware whether or not they *mean* their choice or resolution. Not only is there a sad lack of finality about their will-act, as in the case of people who hesitate, but also there is a strange ignorance as to what their state of will is.

An example will perhaps make this matter clearer.

Let us suppose that a friend, A, is thinking

99

of writing a letter to a man called B. He says to you: "I'm going to write to B to-day." A few moments later he says: "By the way, I don't think I'll write to B to-day, as I'm too busy, and to-morrow will do as well." After a minute or two he begins again, and you listen impatiently: "I think I'll write to-day, all the same, as otherwise B will think it queer, and may get the idea that I'm offended with him. Yes, I'll certainly write to-day." You listen quietly for another announcement, as you somehow now feel that A is quite likely to change his mind once more. Sure enough, after a certain interval, you hear him speak with a tone of petulance: "Look, although I made up my mind to write to B to-day, I'm not going to do so. On the whole, it is better to wait till to-morrow, as I shall be in town this evening, and I may be able to call on him."

Such instances of changes of mind are, we all know, very frequent. There is one point in them worthy of remark and of considerable importance. It is this: Each change, however pitiful, brings one nearer to the climax. Each change is expressed with a growing finality, and there seems to be really a slight, however slight, increase of determination in each new decision. This fact strengthens the supposition that it is only gradually and bit by bit that the indecisive person comes to know his own will in a matter of this kind. No doubt the will was at work but it was working unknown to the person's self, and in too indefinitive and uncertain a way.

There are many other types of will-maladies which merit attention, but on which we cannot now dwell. Some wills are over-confident, some are too timorous and too prone to qualify every resolution made.[6] Other wills are injured by an excessive tendency towards automatism. However, we must now turn to consider the causes of will-maladies.

[6] "In the irresolute," writes Professor James, "all decisions are provisional and liable to be reversed; in the resolute they are settled once for all and not disturbed again."

SECTION VIII

CAUSES OF WILL-MALADIES

SECTION VIII

CAUSES OF WILL-MALADIES

PRESCINDING from character as conditioned by heredity, the factors conditioning the efficiency of will may be divided into two classes, physical and psychical. The "physical factors" affect the will through the body, and the "psychical factors" affect it through the soul. It is only when body and soul are in normal condition that the will is perfectly normal. It may be well, now, to enumerate some of these factors; first, *the physical,* and, secondly, *the psychical.* Among the former we find:

(1) *Ill-health and bodily suffering.*—Through ill-health and suffering the strength and physical energy of the body is diminished, and the body fails to co-operate well with the will. The will seems debilitated as well as the body, and hence it is, that men of strong character, when imprisoned in unwholesome dungeons, starved, and ill-treated, have been often reduced to submission; while they never would have given in

had they been in good health and well treated.

(2) *Fatigue.*—Physical fatigue also so exhausts the strength of the body that it is unable often to co-operate with volitional effort. The effort expended in climbing, say, a high mountain, or walking a long journey, reduces one to a condition of quasi-moral weakness. The will then seems somewhat less well able to make an effort or to exercise control. Hence, in part, the volitional difficulty of getting up to continue a long journey when one is already tired out.

(3) *Locality, climate, hour of the day.*—As animals *who dwell* we are much affected by our physical surroundings. We adapt ourselves unconsciously to our environment. We grow gay or sad, energetic or lethargic, according as hour and weather and scenery affect us. The mad hilarity of the mountain-top is as unreal as the heavy moodiness of the swamp. The tingling gayness of the bright morning is as fictitious as the dull *ennui* of the cold, wet afternoon. Still the will, as the body, is affected by and re-acts to such stimuli.[1]

---

[1] An interesting quotation from St. Teresa may here be given (*Vide,* "Life," p. 114): "Such is our melancholy condition on this earth. As long as our poor soul remains united to this mortal body, it is a prisoner and shares the infirmities of the body. *It is affected by the weather and by*

(4) *Physical Exercise.*—During violent physical exercise, as riding, racing, or playing football, when both body and mind are excited, the will is less capable of normal activity. Still less is the will capable of normal control in a fierce fight, when passion is inspiring our utmost physical efforts.

(5) Other physical conditions also interfere with or affect will-functioning. For instance, to be held or tied so as to be unable to breathe and move normally. For to every volitional act, a bodily movement, however slight, corresponds. Now, if the latter is prevented or curtailed, a certain jar occurs in the functioning of the will.

The psychical factors conditioning the activity of the will are manifold. Some of the more important deserve mention:

(1) *Passion.*—Mental excitement and passion of all kinds, together with such moods as melancholy, despair, or great hilarity, interfere with good willing. If we are under the influence of strong emotion, or if we feel the glow of enthusiasm and excitement, we are in a bad

variations of health, and it often finds itself without any fault on its part incapable of doing what it would like to do. . . . Forcing only aggravates and prolongs the evil. Such persons ought to understand that they are ill.''

condition for willing. At such a time it would be foolish to make an important choice or decision. Excitement may be described as a kind of poison. The body and mind are reduced to an abnormal state, and to some extent incapacitated. The will, the most sensitive of spiritual functions, feels the effect most.

(2) *Restlessness of mind.*—Often some of our mental faculties are hyperactive. It may be that a mad stream of fantastic images is whirling through our minds, or that our brains are working feverishly at some problem. Perhaps, through worry, thoughts or fears are recurring again and again, and our minds are restless and agitated. If so, the will has but a poor chance of functioning normally.

(3) *Lethargy of mind.*—Often we feel our minds dull and slow and empty. No thoughts or images will come. A heavy inertia seems to take possession of us, and we grow apathetic and stupid. Such a condition is, likewise, unsuitable for willing.

(4) *Influence of other Wills.*—The silent influence of other wills, whether hypnotic, or telepathic, or simply the ordinary influence of example, reduces our wills to a slightly abnormal state. We are caught and interested by some other mind, and are led hither and

thither, over hills and across seas, soothed, consoled, or excited. We feel ourselves bound and held somewhat by an alien will. We realise that will moves will; that will is subject to will; that will tends to harmonise with and to move in sympathy with will. When we feel ourselves thus subject to some other will, we need to be doubly cautious before making a choice or a decision.

(5) *Inactivity of Will.*—If for some reason, or simply through neglect, we have failed to exercise our wills for some time, if we have lived without making uphill efforts, and without exercising much self-control, we shall find our wills in part atrophied. Our chief instrument has been out of use and has grown rusty, and consequently it is less likely now to function satisfactorily.

Many other psychical factors influence the will, above all the various habits of thought or feeling which we have acquired. On these, however, it is not necessary to dwell here.

As regards the causes of will-maladies which are of such a kind that they may be removed, three in particular are worthy of attention.

(1) *Want of Exercise.*—It is obvious that unless the will is duly and scientifically exercised

it will, like other faculties, fall into a kind of decay.

(2) *Want of Knowledge of the Will.*—Unless we have a certain knowledge of how the will works, and of how to make choices and resolutions well, it is obvious that we shall misuse the will. Were we to exercise the memory indiscriminately without any knowledge of its nature and capabilities, it would beyond doubt be injured and perhaps permanently destroyed. This, indeed, happens in many cases. And it is a matter of common knowledge that it is owing to the over-burdening and over-working of the memory in modern educational systems that so many men find themselves, while still in the prime of life, incapable of retaining with accuracy proper names and figures.

Want of knowledge of will-psychology leads to our neglect of calling up to the help of the will our other psychical resources. Indeed, the work of the will would, as M. Payot points out, be enormously lightened and facilitated, if we had the art of using the intellect and the emotions in conjunction with the will, while Professor Förster well writes:

"Many young people are apt to be depressed by a continual breaking down of self-control and by failure of their oft-renewed good inten-

110

tions. Frequently these unfortunate results occur *because they do not understand the psychology of will-power.*" [2]

(3) *Want of Confidence in the Will.*—This cause is of course subsidiary to the last, for the reason that a true knowledge of the will would mean immense confidence in its powers. But, of itself, it is so important that it merits to be put down as a special cause.

Many will-maladies would disappear if only we trusted in the will. Its native force is so great, its recuperative power is so sure, and its resources are so unlimited that it is capable of achieving wonderful results. All that is needed is a firm confidence in it. It is, as we have said, our highest and most perfect faculty. It is the best thing we have, and the most effective weapon that we wield. It alone can develop itself. As we saw, it cannot be trained or perfected from without. It alone can cure its own maladies. The one essential thing is, however, that we should place trust and confidence in it.

Considering these three causes of will-maladies together, (1) want of exercise, (2) want of knowledge, and (3) want of confidence, it is our object in this volume to put our

[2] "Marriage and the Sex Problem," p. 177.

readers in the way of removing them by pro-
posing a system of will-exercises, by pointing
out a practical method for studying the will,
and by endeavouring in various ways to show
the power and force of the will.

SECTION IX
METHODS OF WILL-TRAINING

SECTION IX

METHODS OF WILL-TRAINING

MANY authors suggest in a general way exercises of self-denial and mortification as a method of will-training. Professor Förster, for example, thus writes: "Let a teacher try, say on a school walk, to put a little will-gymnastics into practice, by encouraging the boys to resist thirst, tiredness, etc. He will be astonished at the interest which such acts of self-conquest will arouse. . . . The teacher must proceed to what we may describe as the 'science of self-control'; he must show how will-power is built up by a gradual process of practice on the smallest things, and how every act of self-conquest in one sphere of life makes the battle easier in all the other spheres. . . .

"Such exercises as the following will be useful: keeping things tidy, refraining from talking, bodily gymnastics, getting up early in the morning, fasting, doing disagreeable things, carefully speaking the truth, performing drudgery (such as energetically working at a new language) with exactitude. Thus a regeneration of will-power becomes possible such as can hardly ever be achieved by direct effort in the direction of the greatest weakness, because here the tradition of failure has already become too powerful." [1]

Professor James, M. Payot, M. Eymieu and others likewise recommend small acts of self-denial as of the greatest importance in building up the will. A quotation from Professor James may perhaps be given. "Keep the faculty of effort alive in you by a little gratuitous exercise every day. That is, be systematically heroic in little unnecessary points; do every day or two something for no other reason than its difficulty, so that when the hour of dire need draws nigh, it may find you not unnerved nor untrained to stand the test. Asceticism of this sort is like the insurance which a man pays on his house and goods. The tax does him no good at the time, and possibly may never bring him a return. But if the fire does come, his having paid it will be his salvation from ruin. So with the man who has daily inured himself to habits of concentrated attention, energetic volition, and self-denial in unnecessary things. He

[1] "Marriage and the Sex Problem," pp. 175-177.

will stand like a tower when everything rocks around him, and his softer fellow-mortals are winnowed like chaff in the blast.''

We have in our second section dwelt at length on the relation of religion to will-training and have shown that ''the only will-training which the plain man undergoes is the will-training which the practice of religion affords.'' We spoke, of course, of systematic will-training. Another indirect method of will-training which merits attention is that of bodily-development-systems.[2]

No doubt bodily exercises are neither planned nor executed with a view to improving the condition of the will, but *de facto* they do so. They are such a perfect form of discipline when properly carried out, that they afford an excellent training ground for the will. And it should be remembered that body and soul are so closely united that, *a priori,* one could affirm, even though it were not, as it is, confirmed by

[2] Père Gillet, O.P., in his work on ''The Education of Character,'' writes, p. 138: ''Moreover in the building up of character, simple but properly-regulated gymnastics play a prominent part. Some have described gymnastics as 'the primary school of the will.' Gymnastics for the body may serve as model for gymnastics for the soul, whose health is subject, with due reservation, to the same laws as those controlling the body.''

117

experience, that such systems as those of Müller or Sandow or Clarke would assuredly improve the will as well as the bodily members.

It occurs to us here to refer to the lectures given in various parts of Ireland and America (and also to the book [3] published recently) by Rev. William Lockington, S.J., which have excited great interest among thinking men. The object of Father Lockington is, primarily, body-training, but his ulterior object is to improve one's output of work. If the body is more fit, the quality and quantity of the work will be better—such is his reasoning, and it is, of course, quite sound. To us, however, his system suggests something further.

It would seem that, indirectly, his exercises have the effect of training and bracing-up the will. The results he achieves are certainly remarkable. Not only are debilitated and dyspeptic men rendered vigorous and healthy, but lethargic and languid characters are smartened up and energised. The psychic as well as the physical in man is improved by his methods— the reason being that *the will is toned up*. This toning-up of the will is due (1) to the fact that the exercises demand regular and per-

[3] "Bodily Health and Spiritual Vigour." Longmans, London.

severing self-sacrifice; (2) that the will being to some extent dependent on the body for its functioning, improves with the improved condition of the body. It works better and more evenly when the body is in sound health.

Father Lockington's system suggests the following two conclusions. First, if our output of work is relative to our bodily state, it is also relative to the condition of our will. Second, if the will is improved by regular exercises devoted merely to improving the bodily condition, it most likely will be all the more improved by regular exercises devoted directly and primarily to improving the will itself.

Now, the chief excellence of Father Lockington's system is its clearness, simplicity, and definiteness. "Any fool can do them." Similarly, exercises designed to train the will should be so clear, simple, and definite that "any fool may do them." It will, we trust, be found that the exercises which we shall suggest will satisfy this condition. Father Lockington's exercises are not in themselves sacred or spiritual, but they are spiritualised when pursued for a high end. Similarly, the exercises we shall suggest will not in themselves be sacred or spiritual, but they will be capable of being spiritualised by those who undertake them for no-

ble motives. Father Lockington asks for faith
and confidence in his system, as the subjective
condition of the exercitant; we, too, shall ask
for faith and confidence in the system to be explained in a later section.

A type of systematic will-training which
would, of course, neither appeal to nor be very
intelligible to the general public is that in force
in Jesuit noviceships. The first two years of
the young Jesuit's life are spent in an elabo-
rately planned system of occupations, exercises, and disciplines, described by Fr. Bernard
Vaughan, S. J., as a "tread-mill," which are
admirably calculated to develop and perfect
the human will. Scope is given alike for ini-
tiative and for self-repression. To create and
to inhibit, to do and to undo, to "toe the line"
and to carry on a spiritual guerilla warfare,
to put forth effort, but well-regulated and well-
calculated effort, in fine to mould and to be
moulded—all this enters into a Jesuit novice's
life. The whole regime is a method of will-
training. It is based on the spiritual exercises,
and inspired by them. It reduces to fact and
action the Ignatian psychology of memory, understanding and will, inter-dependent, mu-
tually helpful, and synthetised.

Professor Sedgwick has well said, "it is im-

possible to estimate the ultimate good to be
derived, in indirect ways, from any bit of mental cultivation that one manages to give oneself.'' Hence no type of will-training is to be
despised as useless, even though it fall far
short of perfection. The discipline of games,
of school-life, of a military career, or of office-
work is in turn useful, and may be made extremely useful, from our point of view. ''In
no respect,'' writes Dr. Oppenheim, ''can a
man show a finer quality of will-power than in
his own private, intimate life. All of you have
an indefinite number of temptations to be one
sort of person while seeming to be another.
. . . Purity of thought, justness and sweetness
of intention, rectitude in personal relations,
charity of opinion, forbearance in shortcom-
ings or seemingly anomalous standards of
others—these are the intrinsic qualities that
stand for nobility of character. And the cultivation of them is the special province of the
Will.'' Everyday life can then be made a
method of will-training, for nothing is outside
the scope of the will.

From the point of view of ''working with
Nature'' the following method of will-training
is suggested.[4] ''A right method of strength-

4 ''Educating to Purity,'' p. 165.

ening one's will is to ask oneself whether one has not really a special bent and aptitude for some intellectual or material occupation, such as music, writing, manual labour, drawing, gardening, or the service of the neighbour. This being ascertained, exert oneself to master that specialty, by performing that work in so careful and faithful a manner that perseverance and exactitude may become a habit, aye, a passion.'' The underlying thought is helpful, but the suggestion conveyed is too general and too vague to be deemed a method, strictly so called.

It is worth while, for a moment, to recall to mind the Greek view of education. It would seem that their conception of Education was in a broad sense "education of the will," or ethical. "We think of education, on the whole," writes Dr. Bernard Bosanquet, "as an intellectual process, as a process of learning a number of things, each of which, on separate grounds, is necessary to be known. The Greek thought of it, on the whole, as a moral process; or rather, he would not have understood you if you had asked him which of the two he supposed it to be. He would have said that the best experience, if due time and opportunity is given for assimilating it, necessarily enters

122

into the tissue of the mind, and determines its feelings and desires no less than its views and ideas.'' The young Greek was certainly not crammed. He seems to have had ample time to assimilate the limited amount of positive matter that was given him. Meanwhile, however, his character was being carefully trained. He was gradually prepared for the ''heroic offering'' which was implied in the oath taken by the Ephebi, the young cadets of Athens of 17 or 18 years of age. The oath ran, ''I will not dishonour my sacred arms; I will not desert my fellow-soldier by whose side I shall be set; I will do battle for my religion and my country whether aided or unaided. I will leave my country not less, but greater and more powerful than she is when committed to me; I will reverently obey the citizens who shall act as judges; I will obey the ordinances which have been established, and which in time to come shall be established, by natural will; and whosoever would destroy or disobey these ordinances, I will not suffer him but I will do battle for them whether aided or unaided; and I will honour the temples where my fathers worshipped; of these things the gods are my witnesses.''

By this oath we can see what was expected

123

of the perfect young Athenian, and we can see
the ideal which was set before education. The
young Athenian should be a man of will, loyal,
consistent, and fearless, one who knew his own
mind, and one who guided his life by a great
purpose. His splendid physique, won by years
of patient drill in dance and warlike exercise,
was the emblem of his well-ordered firm-set
will. And his reverence for the gods was wed-
ded to a calm and manly pursuit of a high
ideal of patriotism.

It is only necessary to refer to Aristotle's
treatment of the virtue of temperance to show
how well the Greeks understood the need of a
voluntary self-restraint of the appetites of
man, and how well they realised that the function of willing is twofold—to put forth efforts,
and to control. Whether or not their educational methods sufficed to develop fully these
qualities of the will it is not our duty to discuss.
In any case they do not seem to have merited,
as do the men of the present day, the implied
censure of Professor Förster. "In every direction," he writes, "we see the value of consistent training in intellectual culture, in music, in physical development; *in the case of will-
power alone all is left to chance.*" [5]

[5] "Marriage and the Sex Problem," p. 174.

In an "Introduction to Psychology," by Professors Loveday and Green, when dealing with the training of character some suggestions are offered which are worthy of attention, though they by no means constitute a method of will-training. These suggestions are mainly threefold.

(1) *Rewards and Punishments*

"Something may be done by direct rewards and punishments, if it is remembered that forcible repression of an undesirable tendency is useless unless a better is fostered in its place."[6]

(2) *Example*

"The young are ingenuously ready to worship heroes and take any pains to copy them."[7]

(3) *Sympathetic Encouragement*

"The most effectual of all means is sympathetic personal encouragement of common interests and of the actual tendencies to different occupations which in numberless different ways take children out of themselves."[8]

[6] p. 249. [7] ibid. [8] ibid.

It will be remarked that these are means of training character *ab extra* (i.e., from without). As such they cannot but fail. Character must be trained from within—"the true object of education is not merely to furnish the instrument but to train the child in using it.[9] No rewards, or example, or encouragement can succeed in doing this. The boy or man must do it for himself. And hence it is that a practical method of will-training must be of such a kind that one and the same person conducts the process and undergoes it at the same time. Mlle. E. Simon[10] has reduced to four headings her method for training the will in children.

(1) *Tendencies towards sensuality must be thwarted in the child* and it must not be allowed to live too softly and luxuriously. It must be hardened by small hardships.

(2) *The child must be taught to observe order* in the externals of its life. "To achieve order one must take pains, and everything that forces one to take pains requires the intervention of, and simultaneously goes to form the will. A child who has been accustomed to order from his earliest years will necessarily de-

[9] op. cit., p. 25.

[10] Paper read at the "International Congress of Moral Education," 1912.

velop later into a man of will; habitual order leads inevitably to the contracting of the habit of willing." [11]

(3) *The spirit of sacrifice must be inculcated in the child.* Sacrifice demands effort, and effort calls for will. "There are certain inconveniences and privations which may be voluntarily embraced, such as the reduction of one's food, one's amusements, one's sleep, etc. The more voluntary this kind of sacrifice is, the greater its merit." [12]

(4) *Interest, encouragement and good example* form the fourth means of helping the child to live the life of the will.

[11] "Pour avoir de l'ordre il faut se gêner et tout ce qui gêne réclame l'intervention de la volonté et la forme en même temps. Un enfant qui aura été habitué à l'ordre dès ses premières années, sera nécessairement plus tard, un homme de volonté; l'habitude de l'ordre fait contracter infailliblement l'habitude de vouloir."

[12] Il y a les souffrances et les privations qui sont de libre choix, comme se retrancher quelque chose dans sa nourriture, dans ses amusements, dans son sommeil, etc. Ce genre de sacrifice est d'autant plus méritoire qu'il est plus libre de notre part."

SECTION X

A NEW METHOD EXPLAINED

SECTION X

A NEW METHOD EXPLAINED [1]

THERE are two fundamental principles on which the system of will-training which we shall presently explain depends. The first of these principles is that the will must be *self-trained;* the second is that the element of *effort* must enter into the will-training.

As regards the first principle, *the onus of training the will rests on oneself.* Will-training cannot be done from outside and by others. It must be done by oneself. The knowledge of will-psychology, indispensable for the efficient carrying out of the exercises, must be gained by personal introspection. To read the introspections of others is not sufficient. We must come to have an intimate, personal knowl-

[1] We call our method a "new" method. This will probably seem presumptuous on our part, as there is really little in our method which was not known before. However, we have ventured to call it "a new method," as it brings together for the first time, and in a way that is somewhat original, old truths and old practices and synthetises them freshly and concretely.

131

edge of the vital facts of our own will. Again the spirit of seriousness and earnestness which must pervade the exercises must come from our own reflections on the necessity and importance of having a strong will. Finally the planning of exercises, the persevering fulfilment of the plans conceived and chosen, together with the spirit of loyal effort to strengthen the will must come from self. All rests in our own hands. Success or failure depends on ourselves. If we take the matter into our own hands we can train our wills. No one else can do this. All depends on self—for the will must be self-trained.

The second principle is that *the element of effort must enter into the exercises*. This effort need not be great, but, as we shall see, it must be well regulated. It is not always an effort to achieve, or to accomplish something. At times it will be an effort to repress and restrain. It is, needless to say, the price we have to pay. It is the cost of will-development. If this outlay is not made, and if this price is not paid, then the will must remain unperfected. The question for us to decide is, whether or not the thing to be bought is worth the price. The price is paid in daily instalments. An effort is called for every day. Not a great effort, or a long-protracted effort, but some slight effort. All depends on the regular payment of the instalments.

There are, now, certain characteristics of our system of exercises which we must treat of in turn, but we shall do so as briefly as possible. These exercises will naturally pass through three phases.

A. The first phase will be educative.

B. The second phase will be curative.

C. The third phase will be that of strengthening and perfecting.

A. The first phase of the will-exercises will be educative, that is, they will be calculated to give the exercitant a good opportunity of studying the will. These exercises will, if introspections are well done, show the exercitant the nature of his own will, and of its maladies. He will come to see clearly how far he is an impulsive type, how far he is indecisive, hesitating, or lethargic. He will have a good test of his power of perseverance, and of the depth and strength of his resolution to take up the work of will-training. The exercitant will experience already some of the immediate effects of will-training in the feeling of "braced-up-ness," and in the phenomena of "élans de volonté." This first phase will also be important inasmuch as it will show the exercitant what will-training entails, and there is little doubt but that already at this point many will be tempted to discontinue the exercises, although convinced of their need to strengthen their wills.

B. The second phase of the exercises will be curative. Having, during the first phase, found out the chief weaknesses of our wills, we now set ourselves to heal and cure them. Henceforth the exercises will be planned so as to counteract the diseased tendencies of the will. If the exercitant finds out that he is intensely impetuous and impulsive, he will invent exercises which will afford a daily effort in self-restraint or patience. These exercises, if introspections are meanwhile well made, will increase his knowledge of the nature of his impetuosity. He will gradually come to discover its causes and conditions and to remove them one by one. It may be more a physical than a psychological weakness in him. If so he will study how far his external habits conduce to it.

Similarly if the exercitant discovers that he is lethargic, slothful and indolent, he will plan exercises which will afford a daily effort in energetic action. He will for at least five minutes a day stir himself to strenuous activity. Meanwhile he will come to understand better his characteristic will-malady.

C. The third phase of the exercises will be that of strengthening and perfecting the will. We suppose now that the exercitant has in turn studied his will-maladies, and has, at least to some extent, cured them. He now sets himself to build up and bring to perfection his own will. He sets about developing fully all its resources, and calling them into play. He exercises his will in various ways. He attains the power of *resolving* with intensity and depth, so that he means with all the power of his soul his resolutions. He attains the power of *choosing* with care, with deliberation, but with absolute finality. He banishes hesitation and indecision utterly from his soul. He grows more consistent, more energetic, more persevering. He aims at becoming a man of strong will, capable of immense efforts, and of heroic endurance. The exercitant with such high aims will still understand that it is by small daily efforts, carefully graduated and perseveringly followed out, that his ideal must be attained.

It is necessary now to consider, one by one,

135

some of the minor characteristics of our system of will-exercises.

CHARACTERISTICS OF THE WILL-EXERCISES

(1) *Systematic Variation*

The exercises must be varied systematically. This does not mean that they must be made harder or easier, or that they must be directed now against this fault and now against that, in quick succession. The object of varying the exercises is that the tasks may constantly have a certain freshness, so that interest may be kept awake, and so that they may not become merely automatic. A period of ten days seems on the whole to be a good length. Each exercise should last for ten days, the tasks being performed each day, without omitting a single day.

(2) *Continuity of tasks*

The daily task should last from five to ten minutes. They should neither be too long nor too short. During those five or ten minutes the task should go on continuously and without interruption. If an interruption occurs

136

the task should be begun again. If we suppose that the task is to drop in, one by one, slowly and deliberately, fifty matches into a match box, each day for ten days. Now if, when we have dropped in twenty matches some one calls us and we have to attend to some other business the task should be begun again after the interruption, and not merely completed. Similarly, if, say, on the fifth day, we forget all about the task, then the whole set of ten tasks should be begun again, and the four that have been completed should be cancelled.

The reason for this is that in the resolution taken at the beginning of each set of tasks, the condition of continuity is implied—"each day for the next ten days, I shall do so and so."

(3) *Simplicity and triviality*

The tasks should be very simple and definite and practical. There should not be the slightest doubt as to what is meant by the resolution taken. No difficult or obscure conditions should be imposed. Only small, common objects, bits of paper, chairs, books, pencils, coins, boxes, and such like things should be used. Again, the tasks should be *trivial*. This may seem strange, but it is an important condition.

The one and only object of the task is to train the will. There should be no ulterior, interested object in the task, for if so, the primary object of will-training will be lost sight of.

Let us suppose for instance that we set ourselves as a daily task to shave very carefully. This in itself is useful and advantageous. Very soon we should find that we were forgetting all about will-training and performing the task simply for its practical advantage.

The one and only object of the task should be to exercise the will for the sake of the will. People will naturally suggest, as a good type of task, to spend five minutes every morning at Sandow's or Müller's exercises of body-training. This, they will say, is a good will-exercise. No doubt such exercises *indirectly* benefit the will, but *the object of our exercises is to benefit the will in the most direct way possible.* Hence it would be utterly inconsistent with the principles of our method to adopt such exercises and for such motives. We do not want to kill two birds with the one stone. We only want to kill one bird with one stone, to exercise the will in some way or other for the sake of the will. What we want is *to build up will by willing* and not by body-development. For this reason our tasks should have no ul-

138

terior practical object. They should be trivial and useless for all other purposes except
for our one sole purpose of will-training. This
point is of so much importance that it is well
to insist upon it. The element of practical advantage in a task would ruin it from the point
of view of will-development. On this point we
tried experiments, that is by choosing tasks
which were in themselves useful. We always
found that, as a result, as far as we could
judge, the task was a failure from the point
of view of will-training.

(4) *Graduated Effort*

The tasks should, as we have seen, be varied,
and should be directed towards certain definite
ends. They should also be very carefully graduated.

It is well, once and for all, to point out that
the tasks need not be hard. In fact, if they
were hard the whole system would be a failure.
First of all, exercitants would experience disgust, and would soon find an excuse for aban-
doning them. Secondly, if they were hard it
would be extremely difficult to pay sufficient
attention to introspection which is an important element of them. *The tasks should, then,*

be easy, that is, they should only require a slight effort. They should continue to be easy, while at the same time becoming just slightly more difficult. The graduation should be extremely slight, almost negligible. Indeed, the very fact of the daily discipline of performing a five or ten minutes' task, and of strengthening one's resolution to carry it out faithfully already requires no inconsiderable effort.

And the fact that some days we are more fatigued, more hurried, or less "keen" about will-training will in itself introduce an element of variation. Nature will secure in her own way many variations. For both mind and body are in themselves subject to many variations. These variations will in turn react in the ease or difficulty with which we face the tasks.

One obvious disadvantage of interspersing hard tasks with easy tasks is this: The will, like the body, is capable of being worked up to a high pitch of training. If a hard task was carried out for ten or twenty days the will would be "enormously worked up." If then very easy tasks succeeded the effect on the will would be injurious and debilitating. It would be too sudden a "cooling." [2] The will

[2] Those who have made "retreats"—spiritual exercises—for four or eight days know very well what this means. Dur-

should if necessary be worked up, and afterwards reduced to normal conditions, by carefully graduated tasks. But there should be a special reason for doing this.

Tasks should be simple, definite, and easy, while being as little monotonous as possible, the whole object being not to punish nor mortify nor weary but to encourage the exercitant to exercise his will, daily and methodically, according to common-sense principles.

(5) *Persevering Effort*

Needless to say, much time is required in order to bring the will to its full perfection. It is not a matter of days or months, but of years. To cure the will fully of all its faults and maladies is the work of a life-time. This, however, does not mean that no immediate good is to be looked for. On the contrary, the good effects of will-exercises will very soon be felt, and an increase of will-power and energy will be experienced before many exercises are completed.

ing "retreats" the will is worked up to a high state of perfection. This of course is in itself excellent, but at the same time it introduces an element of danger. For if we quit the "retreat" and return at once to a careless or lax spiritual life, we shall not only undo the good of the "retreat," but shall probably fall to a lower spiritual level than before.

There is one consolation, too, in the carrying out of these tasks. Not a jot or tittle of the effort expended will be lost or wasted. All is deposited in a very safe bank. What Professor Sedgwick has said of mind-culture is equally true of will-culture: "It is impossible to estimate the ultimate good to be derived in indirect ways from any bit of mental cultivation that one manages to give oneself." Not only is nothing lost, but a profit which bears an analogy to compound interest, is derived. The will is not only laying by a supply of will-power, but by its very exercises it is increasing its own efficiency in winning will-power. The progression is geometrical. *It adds to itself its own newly-acquired will-power, and thus strengthened, it gains more and more.*

Time, however, as we have said, is needed in order that the will may be fully trained, and thus much perseverance is called for. To understand the need for perseverance it is necessary to consider that in will-training there is always a "general" and a "particular" resolution.

The "general" resolution, which is implicit, is the resolution to take up the work of will-training, and to persevere faithfully in it. The "particular" resolution is that which determines on the precise task for these ten days in which we find ourselves.

Now the perseverance brought into play by the "general," or major, resolution is, of itself, of inestimable value in the training of the will. It calls for no small sum of will-power. And it was because of it that we said that will-power is required in will-training— that we need will, in order to train the will. Having thus far considered the characteristics of our method of will-training, we shall in our next section give some concrete examples of will-tasks, and of the technique connected therewith.

SECTION XI

THE TECHNIQUE OF THE NEW METHOD

SECTION XI

THE TECHNIQUE OF THE NEW METHOD

THE technique of the exercises may now be described. It is extremely simple, and there is no glamour of mystery about it. The essentials for each experiment are: a quiet room where they may be carried on without interruption; a watch to keep the time of duration and the hour at which the experiment takes place; and a note-book wherein to enter the Introspections. The articles used in the tasks should be of the simplest kind and such as every one has at hand.

To begin the experiments, the date and hour are written into the note-book, together with the *resolution,* which is at the same time formally made. Then the task is duly carried out, and the exercitant writes into the note-book his introspection.

As these directions may be hard to understand without a concrete example, we propose to give in full one or two exercises of a subject who actually made them. The first exercise we shall give (which was for seven days, not for ten) naturally belongs to *the educative phase,* as it was the very first exercise of this subject. It was as follows:

EXERCISE I

Resolution, August 11, 1913.
> *"Each day, for the next seven days, I will stand on a chair, here in my room, for ten consecutive minutes, and I will try to do so contentedly."*

I. *August 11* (From 10 to 10:10 P. M.)

Introspection.
> "Exercise a little strange and unnatural. Had to smile, or cross my arms and stand akimbo in order to feel *contented.* Time went quickly and pleasantly. Found it hard to keep 'willing contentment' and doing nothing. Of course, I had distracting thoughts, e. g., 'What would this experiment lead to? Would any one come in?' The ticking of my watch was annoying. I felt very free doing my own sweet will."

148

II. *August 12* (From 11:11 to 11:21 A. M.)

Introspection.

"Task passed easily and not unpleasantly. Had feeling of contentment and even of a kind of pride or manfulness in fulfilling my will. I felt, too, *braced up,* not merely in my mind, but also physically by the mere exercise of willing and fulfilling my resolution. At one moment I feared interruption (hearing a step outside my room) but was very glad when it passed by. Had distractions and felt a little unnatural."

III. *August 13* (From 10:22 to 10:32 A. M.)

Introspection.

"Task passed quickly and not unpleasantly, although there is a certain strain in maintaining contentment of mind. *I experienced a feeling of power and resourcefulness* in fulfilling this self-imposed task. Joy and strength are felt in willing and fulfilling one's will. The exercise certainly tones me up morally and awakens a sense of nobility and manfulness. I maintain an attitude, not of submission to the resolution, and of resignation, but rather of actively willing to be doing what I am doing, and it is this which gives satisfaction. I find, too, in my mind a consolation from the thought that the exercise is legitimate and profitable.''

IV. *August 14* (From 9:59½ to 10:09½ A. M.) *Introspection.*

''Task passed quietly; a little tedious and tiring. Mental satisfaction felt in fulfilling resolution. I experienced again that *feeling of resourcefulness or manfulness* in carrying out my will—but think that to some extent I am bracing myself up in addition to willing contentment. The exercise certainly tones me up and awakens a pronounced sense of strength and virility.

''It struck me (as a distraction) how important it is for us to be aware of our own will-force and will-power, in such matters as keeping resolutions. It increases self-confidence, self-reliance, and helps us to face the work of winning self-control more bravely.''

V. *August 15* (From 9:55½ to 10:05½ A. M.) *Introspection.*

''Task passed quietly and evenly. Feeling of satisfaction in fulfilling resolution. I felt it possible to intensify my will-effort (*élan de volonté*) by embracing and identifying myself with the resolution more and more. I experienced again but more obscurely that feeling of manfulness and strength in willing my will. My interest waned a little towards the latter half of the task."

VI. *August 16* (From 10:07 to 10:17 A. M.)

Introspection.

"Task passed quietly and easily. Not much strain. 'Willing contentment' comes perhaps more easily and more quietly. Somewhat distressed at times and feel less braced up. The task is becoming habitual. Evidently it will be necessary to change the task often, in order to secure the bracing-up feeling. I tried to intensify my will-effort in performing the task but do not know if I succeeded. I experienced a certain sense of being in harmony with a law (i. e., my resolution)."

VII. *August 17* (From 10:12 to 10:22 A. M.)

Introspection.

"Task passed quietly and fairly quickly. Some distractions and less 'exciting.' I felt

151

satisfaction, not so much *sensible* as *mental,* in fulfilling my resolution. Also I experienced a modest sense of strength and power in having been as good as my word. The feeling of being 'braced up' was much less marked—the effort at 'contentment' came much easier. There was no feeling of ennui or monotony.''

  .   .   .   .

At the end of each exercise it is well to append remarks about the exercises as a whole, such as the following:

Notes on Exercise I

(1) A good exercise, simple and easy, but perhaps slightly too long.

(2) I fulfilled it without disgust, hesitation, or difficulty.

(3) I think it tended to tone up my will—especially during the first three or four days.

(4) I think it helps me to understand and realise that I have the power to carry out resolutions faithfully.

(5) I think it adds, slightly at least, to my sense of self-confidence.

  .   .   .   .

Before recording another exercise of this subject it may be well to make a few observations at this point.

The tasks prove to be extremely interesting to the exercitants when they acquire a certain facility in introspecting. They delight to watch and record the various movements and impulses of the mind and will. This work of analysis and observation is, of course, itself an excellent discipline. Nothing stimulates the mind so much as the observation of its own wonderful, complex, subtle activities. The psychological sense, like the poetic sense, affords unending delight to the happy possessor. The poet finds his pleasure and happiness in studying the external works of nature, and in interpreting her moods and her strange achievements. The psychologist finds nature in his own mind, and there he feasts on beauties as rich and varied as those of the Alps, Yellowstone Park or Killarney.

The exercise which we have recorded was one *of purely educative interest*. The subject was simply finding out for himself some will-phenomena, and preparing to be able to discover his own will-maladies. In the exercise which we shall now record, the subject is in the beginning of *the curative stage*. He has found

153

out that the chief fault of his will is some form of impetuosity, and he is now undertaking an exercise in which a certain self-control is called for. Meanwhile he is studying the various symptoms of his malady. The task reveals to him the restlessness and feverishness of his will, and he feels it a veritable torture to curb his impetuousness.

As the experiments proceed, a certain improvement and increase of control may be noticed, and the task becomes a little less hard.

.   .   .   .

The exercise lasted from November 13, 1913, till November 22, inclusive, and usually occupied ten minutes. The material consisted of (1) a hundred small bits of card-board, each about the size of a dime; (2) a small tin box about three inches high, in which the bits of card-board were dropped, one by one; and (3) a table on which the bits of card-board were deposited in a heap beside the box.

EXERCISE XI

Resolution, November 13, 1913.

> *"Each day for the next ten days I shall calmly and deliberately, without haste,*

*replace in the box (one by one) the hun-
dred bits of card-board."*

I. *November 13* (From 10:55 to 11:07 P. M.)

Introspection.
"Task tiresome, long, and difficult. It seems
to me impossible to act calmly and without
haste—*even when moving slowly.* My actions are jerky and impetuous. There is an
uneasy tension in my movements. I can't do
a thing in a frigid, calm way. The will is
strained, quietly and tediously, by this task.
It is bracing in another kind of way. The
will achieves new powers. For me the power
of patient action is non-existent. This exercise gives me an insight into the short-com-
ings of my own will. I see clearly my impetuosity and impulsiveness—a heated ex-
citability in my will and temperament."

II. *November 14* (From 9:04 to 9:15 P. M.)

Introspection.
"Task very hard; the hardest and most wor-
rying and disagreeable yet. Here the will
finds not only *the what* but also *the how.*
Everything strives against this slow, waste-
155

ful, wearisome dropping in, one by one, of the pieces of paper. Why not do them fast? Hurry up! It is against my whole nature to go slowly; forehead, fingers, chest and eyes, all strain for quicker action. Every little uncontrolled movement degenerates into a jerk and a rush. It is so hard to go slowly and deliberately. I feel worried, angry, unhappy, uncomfortable. It is distressing. *Still the victory is won and I am somewhat braced up.* But it is not a gracious victory. I took it in bad part."

III. *November 15* (From 9:20 to 9:32 P. M.)

Introspection.

"Task very hard; a constant strain. Even when going slowly my will 'wants me to go as fast as ever I can while going slowly.' I am tempted to think it is impossible constitutionally for an impulsive character to act slowly and deliberately. Certainly I feel it utterly against the grain. Each piece of paper was the occasion of a fresh struggle. The task is tiring. I feel mentally and morally braced up. The after-effects of this task are considerable. Introspection is a little difficult. It is a severe test of will-patience.

156

I experienced a feeling of tension in the fore-head—a hot, worried feeling."

IV. *November 16* (From 9:45½ to 9:56½ p. m.)

Introspection.

"Task quiet, monotonous. At times I was very distracted. I put in the bits of paper in a semi-mechanical way. I find that when I forget what I am about and grow careless the opposition from impulsiveness and impetuosity disappears. The will calls up opposition to itself. The will-act, or *élan*, tonight, was very weak and the opposition almost nil. I was tired and sleepy. The exercise did not seem so hard as before for the reason that I felt indifferent to it. I didn't care much. I would not have dreamed, however, of omitting the task or of changing it into something easier."

V. *November 17* (From 9:09½ to 9:19½ p. m.)

Introspection.

"Task very unpleasant, distasteful, wearisome, and distressing. I dislike this task very much. It depresses me, too. It is painful, perhaps because it goes against my natural tendency to impetuosity. I find no pleasure in dropping in slowly, one by one, the pieces of paper. I have to watch myself lest I jerk and do it hastily. I experienced a tired headachy feeling. I find it hard to breathe evenly and was distracted. For a moment I cheered myself up, saying, 'I shall do it contentedly,' but this feeling of contentment soon disappeared. I feel all the same braced up *mentally*, not *physically*. It is a will-exercise. The characteristic will-feeling was not much in evidence. Introspection was a little hard.''

VI. *November 18* (From 9:00½ to 9:11½ P. M.)

Introspection.

''Task was quiet, slow, monotonous and very hard. I watched my hand working slowly and said, 'Look how strong my will is and how much my hand is subject to my will.' This point of view aroused my will; it felt more active; braced up; and controlled the working of my hand more deliberately and easily afterwards. Will-feeling was obscurely present. The task was headachy and a little depressing. Distractions but no temptations to abandon the task. I felt at times that it was veritably 'will-training.' It is a good exercise for the will. A steady resolve to fulfil the task fills my mind."

VII. *November 19* (From 9:13½ to 9:23 P. M.)

Introspection.

"Task passed quietly. Less unpleasant. I was conscious as I watched my hand slowly and obediently working, (1) of the power of the will, (2) of a certain deep sense of power and strength. I put in the pieces calmly, slowly, and deliberately. The will controlled the action better while I watched my hand working. Braced up by the task. Will-feeling present, but not very openly. Task was less disagreeable, but it is still long and hard. I find myself saying, 'Next task will be shorter.' My will faces the definite (definitive) task before it and concentrates on that. Therein lies its strength."

VIII. *November 20* (From 5:15 to 5:25½ P. M.)

Introspection.

"Task slow and uninteresting. Felt all the same that I was not going slow enough; that I was not fully overcoming my will. I often,

159

in such things, feel that somehow my will is managing to escape me, and I am not quite 'smashing' at it, but missing my aim a little. Feel anxious to have the task finished. At times I felt braced up and proud to be exercising my will. As I looked down at my hand, slowly and obediently working, I was struck by the power of will, by its supremacy. The ultimate idea of will-training has been less in my mind the last few days, and the task has been less pleasant and good-humoured."

IX. *November 21* (From 4:56 to 5:07½ P. M.)

Introspection.

"Task passed quietly; distracted, or rather uninterested. I feel that the 'will-bent,' or 'determination' given in the beginning of the task pervades it to the end, and secures its fulfilment. I felt the *seriousness* and *significance* of the task. Braced up somewhat; will-feeling was appreciably present. A good task, but it becomes somewhat mechanical and the strain lessens. A sense of the power of the will was present. The more definite the resolution, the more easily the will seems to work. The 'end' or 'resolution' seems to

160

have a certain compelling force on the will.
It keeps the will up to the mark. The 'will'
and the 'end' act and react on each other.''

X. *November 22* (From 6:22 to 6:33 P. M.)

Introspection.

''Task was quiet; much more interesting and
instructive. Will-feeling was present. Will
was toned up; braced up. I observed (1)
that I had been going too slow before, and
that was not in the resolution. (2) The will
should insist on the action running along the
lines of (or between the walls of) the resolution. (3) Willing should be closely connected with mind—it should be the faithful
and precise fulfilling of the resolution—not
more nor less. (4) It is as much impetuosity to go (e. g., in this task) too slow as too
fast, for the essence of impetuosity is to give
way to or be driven before motives. And to
go too slow, in this task, as well as to go
too fast, is to be driven before motives. (5)
Self-control and self-command means that
the will drives the human machine exactly
and precisely along predetermined lines.
Will is to control activity duly; well-regulated effort is its proper outcome.''

161

As regards introspections, such as those which we have given as examples, it must be remembered that they are always open to the charge of subjectivity and auto-suggestion. Indeed, it may readily be admitted that all introspection is to some extent coloured by fancy, and subjective. It is impossible to be perfectly objective when introspecting. It is impossible to be exact and complete in describing internal phenomena.

Still, though introspection is a faulty method of observation, it is by no means worthless. It is the method given us by nature. It is the only method we have of finding out what goes on within us. And it can, if used with caution, be wonderfully efficient. In fine, it is a method that we cannot dispense with, and that we cannot disregard, but that, at the same time, we cannot wholly trust.

For our purpose, however, it is perfectly satisfactory and sufficiently accurate. For it affords us a good practical knowledge of the phenomena of the will, of its impulses, activities, and weaknesses.

SECTION XII

A TENTATIVE SCHEME OF EXERCISES

SECTION XII

A TENTATIVE SCHEME OF EXERCISES

In the two foregoing sections we have given examples of the exercises which we recommend with a view to will-training, and we have described at length the method and characteristics of these exercises.

If followed out they are calculated not only to keep the will healthy and energetic, but to develop its resources and cure its defects. By willing, the will grows stronger. By willing, the will comes to build up will-power. Above all, by willing will, the will builds up the will. This must be the primary characteristic of the will-task, that in it the will is willing will.

Another important characteristic of these will-tasks is that in them the will focuses its strength on some small, definite object to be achieved. It learns "to get a thing done," "to carry out" something. It learns to act, and to achieve. The feeling of being able to accomplish something that lies before us, however trivial it may be, awakens in us a new confidence and sense of power. "At least," we say to ourselves, having faithfully performed a few exercises, "there are some things I can do, there are some resolutions I can keep." Our sense of strength grows. We face new tasks and difficulties in a bolder, braver spirit. We find ourselves "braced up," and we presently discover that the will is really able to carry us over big obstacles. Above all, we shall not be tempted to give way to despair, and say with so many men, young and old, "I have no longer any will. I simply can't help it."

As regards the details of the method we suggest, everything must be regarded as purely tentative. *Our method is capable of being applied in various ways to suit various situations.* We do not wish it to be considered rigid. It should be modified and changed to suit circumstances. As regards the length of time, the nature of the tasks, the writing out of all or only of some introspections, the performing the tasks every day, or only three times a week —all such details must be arranged by the exercitant himself. We only wish to suggest an outline, in a purely tentative way, of a method of will-training on what we consider common-sense lines.

166

As it may be helpful to some to suggest a few exercises to start with, we shall do so—although it would be more in accordance with our wishes to leave the determining of the particular tasks entirely to the exercitant himself. However, for convenience' sake, we shall suggest a few.

I.   PRELIMINARY EXERCISES

These exercises are suitable for what we have called the Educative Phase.

I.   To stand on a chair for five minutes with arms crossed.[1]

II.   To repeat quietly and aloud, "I *will* do *this*," keeping time with rhythmic movements of a stick or ruler for five minutes.

III.   To hold hands upstretched vertically for five minutes.

IV.   To walk to and fro in room, touching in turn say a clock on the mantelpiece and a particular pane of glass for five minutes.

[1] Each task should be performed each day for ten consecutive days. Then another task should be begun. The will should be exercised during the five minutes in earnest will-acts, so that the task should be done willfully and contentedly.

167

V. To keep eyes steadily fixed on a small object for five minutes.

VI. To keep one hand in a basin of cold water for five minutes.

VII. To count and recount aloud some dozen small objects for five minutes.

VIII. To listen to the ticking of a clock or watch, making some definite movement at every fifth tick.

IX. To get up on and get down from a chair thirty times.

X. To read aloud, forwards and backwards, a paragraph from a book for five minutes.

．　　．　　．　　．　　．　　．　　．

It may be well here to make a few remarks. These tasks are merely *suggestive* of the type to be employed. They are designedly trivial and a little strange. If the element of *strangeness* did not enter in, it would be hard to keep interest and attention awake. It is supposed, of course, that the will will be occupied during each task *in a steady resolve* to fulfil the conditions fully. Indeed, the tasks as given above only represent the *external* part of the exercise. The *internal* part and the most important part, is the activity of the will *in willing resolutely and contentedly*. The triviality of the tasks allows of their being indefinitely varied. Numberless tasks of such a kind can easily be imagined. At times old tasks may with profit be repeated. Then the old and new introspections should be compared.

The tasks given above are all *positive*. They consist in accomplishing something during a certain fixed time. But another kind of task—*negative tasks*—will at once suggest themselves. They will consist in avoiding something during a longer or indefinite time. For instance, I might resolve during the next ten days never to use a pencil, or never to enter a certain room, or never to step on a particular doormat. These negative tasks will also be of great utility.

To one point, in particular, attention must be drawn. *It is all-important to get the will to will with more and more intensity*. The excercitant should see to this above all. He should try to gauge the strength of his will-acts and should try to render them more and more deep and earnest. In this way he will acquire the power of making stronger and stronger resolutions.

169

II. THE CURATIVE PHASE

When the exercitant considers that he has a sufficiently accurate knowledge of his will and of its weaknesses he will begin to invent exercises calculated to benefit his will. A few examples may be given—merely tentatively—as suitable for "impetuous" wills.

Exercises for an "Impetuous" Will

I. To replace in a box, very slowly and deliberately, one hundred matches or bits of paper.

II. To write out, very slowly and carefully, fifty times the words, "I will train my will."

III. To turn over, slowly and quietly, all the leaves of a book (about 200 pages).

IV. To stand for five minutes in as complete a condition of listlessness and lethargy as possible.

V. To swing the arms over the head very slowly and deliberately for five minutes.

VI. To watch the movement of the second-hand of a clock or watch, and to pro-

nounce some word slowly at the com-
pletion of each minute.

VII. To draw on a piece of paper, very slowly and painstakingly, parallel lines
for five minutes.

VIII. To count aloud, slowly, up to two hundred.

IX. To put on and take off a pair of gloves
(or brush a hat) very slowly and deliberately for five minutes.

X. To move a chair from one side of the
room to the other, very slowly for five
minutes.

N. B. These exercises can be readily be adapted to suit a "lethargic" type of will.

.   .   .   .

The *tasks* should be most exactly carried out.
They should neither be longer nor shorter, nor
harder nor easier, nor swifter nor slower, than
the stipulated amount. The predetermined
bounds should be most faithfully observed, and
during the period of the tasks no change what-
soever should be made. Some exercises of a
more difficult kind may at times be tried. Those
we have spoken of deal with external movements and acts, but it is possible to have good
exercises dealing with what is psychical and
internal. For instance, if we place a watch

171

well within ear-shot, so that *we can hear it ticking most distinctly*. Then, for five minutes, try by energetically distracting the attention (without of course making noise or moving externally) to no longer hear the ticking of the watch. This is a most interesting exercise, though very difficult and distressing.[1]

Exercises such as we have suggested afford an excellent system of self-discipline. Ascetics, as we know, inflict severe pain on their bodies by various means; and harshly refuse the dearest yearnings of their hearts. *They go against their own will* in a hundred different ways in order to have complete control of themselves. Such mortification is so admirable and so essential that in every age the Church has taught and practised it. It is the "Deny yourself" of the Gospel. It is the "hard word" to which we must all listen.

Now, self-discipline, to be really effective, must be systematic, moderate, and well-conceived. It can adopt a thousand different forms. The form, indeed, matters little. The essence is that it should cost not too much, nor

[1] This exercise in *deliberate distraction of attention* is worthy of special study in view of the question which arises with regard to sensuality (*Vide,* Section XIV), as to how far the will can control attention and draw it away from something which holds it strongly.

too little—but that it should cost just so much as, given various circumstances relative to the person, will be helpful to that person's will. *For the grand object of self-discipline is, in reality, to brace up the human will for the struggle of the moral life.*

Now, the exercises which we suggest are, of course, designed to brace up the human will. They are systematic and moderate and should be conceived so as to suit well all relative circumstances. *They are not designed to cause physical pain,* although they entail effort and expenditure of physical strength. They are planned to cost the will some effort. They cost, not too much nor too little, but just enough, given the circumstances of the case.

To strengthen the will, and to render it energetic, ready, persevering and consistent, some system of exercises is obviously necessary. The education of the will must not be left to chance. Nor, indeed, can it be left to others. As we have already seen, *it must be carried out by ourselves.* It must be carried out, too, in accordance with the knowledge we can ourselves acquire of our own wills. *Self-study and self-discipline must then go hand-in-hand.* Time, effort, and patience is the price to be paid. The system to be followed is sim-

173

ple, practical and clear. There is no mystery and there is no short-cut. The goal to reach is self-mastery, personal power and energy of character. The way is long, but the goal is worth winning.[2]

[2] As regards the third phase, that of *Strengthening and Perfecting the Will,* we leave the planning of exercises entirely to the exercitant himself. The exercises will naturally be somewhat harder and more trying than those hitherto spoken of.

SECTION XIII

THE WILL AND HABIT

SECTION XIII

THE WILL AND HABIT

It is necessary, at this point, having explained our proposed method of will-training, to discuss the question of habit, for in habit the will, on the one hand, finds its chief obstacle, and on the other hand its chief auxiliary. To overcome habits which are injurious to character is the first important work of the will, and to form habits calculated to secure and perpetuate its victories is the second important work of the will.

In general, we may say that our lives are one vast mass of habits. Almost all we do is done according to habits formed at different times. We get up, dress, eat, talk, walk, and work by habit. The formation of these habits is the characteristic work of the will. Many of them, good or bad, are swiftly made. Oftentimes, one or two repetitions of the same act suffice to form a habit. The oftener these acts are re-

peated, the stronger grows the habit, and the
more deeply it is embedded in our nature. The
older and stronger a habit is, the harder it is
to give it up or break through it, in other words
the more difficult it is to form an antagonistic
habit. For the only way to lay aside one habit
is by replacing it by another. "All our life,"
writes Professor James, "so far as it has definite form, is but a mass of habits—practical,
emotional, and intellectual—systematically organised for our weal or woe, and bearing us ir-
resistibly toward our destiny, whatever the
latter may be."[1]

It is in the dual principle of man that is found
the reason why to such an extent we are creatures of habit, "imitators and copiers of our
past selves." We are formed of matter and
spirit, of body and soul, capable of bearing
physical impressions in our bodies, and as
liable to be "bent" or "curved" as the twig of
a tree or the leaf of a book. For just as the
twisting of a piece of wire gives it a physical
tendency to take up a certain shape, so the
straining of our muscles or the curving of our
lips to form a peculiar smile, or the furrowing
of our brows in a certain way, secures that
these parts are shaped just as the piece of wire

[1] "Talks to Teachers," p. 64.

is shaped. Again, although intellect and will are spiritual functions, still they also are immersed in matter, and to every movement of theirs, corresponds a movement in the brain, that is, in their material correlative. And so it is that habits of thought and habits of willing can be formed, at least in this sense, that physical impressions are traced somehow and somewhere in the brain which correspond to these acts of intellect and will. In the will, in particular, in choice-acts which have become habitual, a certain kind of "structure" seems to persist in such a way that motives take a habitual course according to it, or according to the nature of the motivation tracks.[2] Will and intellect can thus form habits, and in addition, as Dr. Carpenter writes, "our nervous systems have grown to the way in which they have been exercised, just as a sheet of paper or a coat, once creased or folded, tends to fall for ever afterwards into the same identical fold."

As we go on in life, we grow more and more like automatic machines. Our habits increase in number and strength. Saint and sinner alike do a hundred things, unconsciously, in

[2] *Vide,* "Motive Force and Motivation Tracks," Longmans, 1911.

the same characteristic old way. Of both types of men we often speak thus: "It's just like him. I knew he'd do that." Everything we do tends to fall under some habit or other, good or bad. This does not mean that we are any the less responsible for our acts, or any the less free. For we are responsible for forming our habits, and even when we act according to habits, there is nothing to show that we are not acting freely. An automatic act does not mean a non-free act. It means an act that takes place with maximal ease, evenness, and economy of volitional effort, owing to similar acts having often been done before. But it neither prescinds from the attention of the mind nor consent of the will. In fine, it never has been shown and never can be shown that what is called, in the broad sense, an automatic act, passes unknown to the mind and unapproved by the will.[3]

[3] *Vide,* "Motive Force and Motivation Tracks," p. 142.

"We understand Automatism in a wide sense, as being the state arrived at by the Will, when it functions, evenly, swiftly, and regularly, and in a manner, more or less independent of conscious attention. We do not imply that consciousness is altogether absent in automatic actions. It seems to us that facts show that there is usually present some trace of consciousness. We quite agree with Mr. Stout ('Manual of Psychology,' p. 109) that, in automatic actions, 'the diversity of attention is probably never absolutely complete. The musician,

We find ourselves, then, as time goes on, with certain inseparable companions—our habits. If they are good habits—cheerfulness, industry, honesty, and temperance—it is well for us. Our lives will be lives of peace and goodness. But if, on the other hand, we allow ourselves to contract bad habits our lot is bound to be wretched.

It is with the object of helping others to form good habits that Professor James formulated certain practical rules, to some of which we shall forthwith refer.

First Maxim.
>   *"We must make our nervous system our ally instead of our enemy."*

Seeing that habits are formed most readily when we are young, we must, writes James, "make automatic and habitual, as early as possible, as many useful actions as we can, and as carefully guard against the growing into ways that are likely to be disadvantageous."

for instance, is more or less aware that he is playing a piece of music, and the absent-minded walker is not utterly oblivious to the fact that he is in a crowded street and in motion. What can be asserted is, that in such cases there is no persistent and discriminating attention to the details of the action.' ''

Second Maxim.

> *"In the acquisition of a new habit or the leaving off of an old one, we must take care to launch ourselves with as strong and decided an initiative as possible."*

Naturally the first days of the life of a new habit are critical. There is danger and difficulty to be faced, and hence, writes James, "accumulate all the possible circumstances which shall reinforce the right motives; put yourself assiduously in conditions that encourage the new way; make engagements incompatible with the old; make a public pledge if the case allows; in short, envelope your resolution with every aid you know. This will give your new beginning such a momentum that the temptation to break down will not occur as soon as it otherwise might; and every day during which a break-down is postponed adds to the chances of its not occurring at all."

Third Maxim.

> *"Never suffer an exception to occur till the new habit is securely rooted in your life."*

Professor Bain points out well the importance of this maxim: "It is necessary above all things," he writes, "in such a situation never to lose a battle. Every gain on the wrong side undoes the effect of many conquests on the right. The essential precaution, therefore, is so to regulate the two opposing powers that the one may have a series of uninterrupted successes, until repetition has fortified it to such a degree as to enable it to cope with the opposition under any circumstances. This is the theoretically best career of mental progress."

Fourth Maxim.

> *"Seize the very first possible opportunity to act on every resolution you make, and on every emotional prompting you may experience in the direction of the habits you aspire to gain."*

The reason for this is that only in *exercising* resolutions are they really made. Then the brain cells and the physiological correlatives of the new resolution get their proper adjustments. "A tendency to act," writes James, "only becomes effectively ingrained in us in proportion to the uninterrupted frequency with which the actions actually occur, and the brain 'grows' to their use. When a resolve or a fine glow of feeling is allowed to evaporate without bearing practical fruit, it is worse than a chance lost."

In this *maxim* Professor James speaks of a *resolution* as though it were the same thing as *habit*. From one point of view there is little difference between the two. The resolution usually precedes the habit. The keeping of the resolution means the formation of the habit. The word *habit*, however, is more general and covers many involuntary kinds of acts which are outside the scope of deliberate resolve.

Fifth Maxim.

> *"Keep the faculty of effort alive in you by a little gratuitous exercise every day."*

This maxim does not refer directly to habit-formation. It suggests merely, in general, a method for toning up the will, so that it may be more likely to stand fast by its good habits.[4]

The evil effects of bad habits are known even to the youngest of us, for we see all around us the social and moral degradation which follows, for example, the drink habit. Medical scientists have shown the swift deterioration

[4] For the quotation in full of James's remarks on this maxim, see above, page 116.

of the nervous system under the influence of alcohol and psychologists have shown the concurrent deterioration of the mental faculties. For the moment we are concerned with the will, and shall dwell only on the evil effects of alcohol on this supreme faculty of man. The will, we have seen, like every other mental faculty, has a material correlative. It may be that this correlative is found in certain movements of the brain-cells; be that as it may, it is proved beyond question that volitional functioning deteriorates according as the alcohol habit grows. The dipsomaniac loses his power of healthy willing. He cannot make the effort required to resist his propensity. He is incapable of calm deliberation. He is in no sense master of himself. He has lost his power of control and his senses and mental powers are dulled. His state is piteous in the extreme, yet, as Mr. Kerr[5] writes, "serious as are the injuries inflicted by intoxicants on the intellectual faculties, the loss of inhibitive capacity is a hundredfold more detrimental. To these must be added the progressive paralysis of the will. The damage done to the understanding is great, but infinitely more terrible are the decrease of control and the benumbing of vo-

[5] Quoted by Professor James.

lition. Many inebriates, as long as they retain consciousness, through all their outbreaks know what they are doing, hate with a perfect hatred their drunken excesses, but are as unable to exert their will as is a terror-stricken animal helpless under the fascination of a boa-constrictor. The moral faculties are even more deadened by the poison than the intellectual. Alcohol is a puissant will-paralyser. Such an inebriate is a captive, retaining the possession of his senses, though these are somewhat dulled, and the will is powerless to make an effort at deliverance. Again and again does he resolve to drink no more, but resolution is overborne by the dominating drink impulse or drink crave. This volitional disablement, this palsy of the will, is a direct effect of a pathological degradation.''

The most pitiful thing about the inebriate is his incapacity to save himself—to make an effort. He longs, often, to be free. He tries to brace up his will. He begs others to help him. He would pay any sum of money to be delivered. He swears a thousand times that he will drink no more. He sobs when he looks at his patient, long-suffering wife, and at the pale, pinched faces of his children. He promises most solemnly that he will be sober henceforth

—he takes his little youngest child in his arms and kisses away his fear and makes him laugh. And then, after all this, after all these good resolves, he goes out and the very first wine-shop that he meets he enters, without the faintest effort at turning away. He falls, while the tears of repentance are still wet on his cheeks.

I shall not enter into details as to the exact effects of alcohol in the system. Suffice it to say that it poisons the blood, and that the blood is no longer able to nourish the nerve-tissues. As a consequence the healthiness and capacity for work of the inebriate diminishes. Just as vigorous health, full pure-blooded fitness, is the optimal condition for making volitional effort, so the nervous debility consequent on intoxication is the worst possible condition for such effort-making. *He* may think, and his friends may think that he could, if he tried, give up drink—but when things have gone far it is all but impossible. Only extraordinary circumstances, and the help of God's grace, can then save him.

It is in presence of such considerations that Professor James writes as follows: "The hell to be endured hereafter, of which Theology tells, is no worse than the hell we make for ourselves in this world by habitually fashioning our characters in the wrong way. Could the young but realise how soon they will become mere walking bundles of habits, they would give more heed to their conduct while in the plastic state. We are spinning our own fates, good or evil, and never to be undone.''

We have seen how habit is founded both in the material and spiritual side of human nature—in the brain-cells and in the facility with which the will itself remakes former decisions or choices. We have seen too the vast significance of habit, its importance for good or for evil. To use Carlyle's words, ''Habit is the deepest law of human nature. It is our supreme strength: if also, in certain circumstances, our miserablest weakness.'' We have also seen the maxims which Professor James has formulated for the benefit of those about to form habits. It now remains for us to see why we are creatures of habit; that is, for what purpose we are by nature made to depend so much on habit.

The first reason is that habit means economy of effort. Towards it all volitional functioning naturally tends. It should not be considered as an evil but as a manifestation of the protective and economising tendency of our nature. It shows that, as Mr. Stout says,[6] "it lies in the essential nature of conation that conative processes should cease, if and so far as their end is attained." Habit has been called a "labour-saving invention" enabling us to get along with less output of strength both in mental and material occupations. In the case of oft-made choices it is most remarkable what an economy takes place, and how habit or automatism enters in. Indeed, the only wasteful tendency is hesitation.

"It suffices for the moment to point out that Hesitation is, so to say, the natural enemy of Volitional Economy.[7] It upsets Automatism, causes the mind to weary itself and waste its force by useless oscillations. It doubles and trebles the usual number of phenomena, lengthens, often immensely, the time-duration, upsets the continuity and evenness of the choice-process and introduces irregularity and inconsistency. On such occasions, Automatism sometimes seems to take revenge, for the Hesitation may close abruptly by the lightning flash of an automatic tendency towards the Critical Zone; the choice thus finishes suddenly, and the Hesitation is stopped."

[6] "Manual of Psychology," p. 111.
[7] "Motive Force and Motivation Tracks, p. 155.

A second reason why nature has made us creatures of habit is for our own safety. At every moment we are saved by our habits from mistakes and mishaps. It is well known that no chauffeur or aëroplanist is safe until he can manage his machine in a perfectly habitual way, until he can almost manage it when asleep. Habit also makes the typist or telegraphist expert. Art must become a habit before perfect security and skill are attained.

Not only is habit economising, and protective, but it also tells for efficiency. It is only the player, to take a commonplace example, who has reduced all his best strokes to perfectly automatic movements, who can be considered a really efficient batsman. For him, as for the motorist and the rest, habit means less fatigue, less risk, and greater accuracy.

There is, of course, a less serious side to the question of habit. Men become, at times, slaves to habits of a very trivial kind. "Schiller [8] could never write with ease unless there were rotting apples in the drawer of his desk from which he could now and then obtain an odour which seemed to him sweet. Wagner required a certain costume before he could compose corresponding parts of his operas. Glad-

[8] "Mental Growth and Control," Oppenheim, p. 153.

stone had different desks for his different activities, so that when he worked on Homer he never sat among the habitual accompaniments of his legislative labours.'' The story of Emmanuel Kant and the button of the Königsberg student is well known. During his lectures, and they were most learned and carefully prepared, he never looked his audience in the face, but always fixed his eye on one member of it. Now, one of his students began to notice that, during lectures, Kant always fixed his eye on him, and kept staring all the time at a certain button of his coat. Well, one day, an unpardonable spirit of levity seized him. Before going into the lecture he took a knife and cut off the mystic button that used to catch Kant's eye. Forthwith he entered the hall and sat down in his accustomed place. As usual the lecture started, and as usual Kant's eye wandered round until it rested on the student, then on his coat, then it sought in vain the missing button. Then Kant stopped. All his lecture quite left him. He blundered and fumbled, and, at last, unable to continue, got up and went out. As regards the overcoming of undesirable habits, two things must be remembered. The first is that the stronger and more efficient one's will is, the easier it will be to make or unmake a habit. The first step, therefore, towards ridding oneself of undesirable habits must be to train the will. The second thing to be remembered is that in will-battles we must apply the principle: *divide et impera.* A small, well-defined resolution must be made which is calculated to run counter to, and undo, the habit of which one wishes to get rid. This small resolution must be tenaciously and persistently observed until a new and better habit is formed. Thus by habit habit will be overcome. We shall close this section by quoting from Dr. Oppenheim's "Mental Growth and Control." [9] "If you want to abolish a habit, and its accumulated circumstances as well, you must grapple with the matter as earnestly as you would with a physical enemy. You must go into the encounter with all tenacity of determination, with all fierceness of resolve,— yea, even with a passion for success that may be called vindictive. No human enemy can be as insidious, as persevering, as unrelenting as an unfavourable habit. It never sleeps, it needs no rest. . . . It is like a parasite that grows with the growth of the supporting body. And like a parasite it can best be killed by violent separation and crushing."

[9] p. 159.

SECTION XIV

THE WILL AND SENSUALITY

SECTION XIV

THE WILL AND SENSUALITY

THE subject of sensuality is not an easy nor an agreeable one to treat of, yet it would be affectation and not modesty to pass over it in silence when writing about will-training. Sensuality, whatever form it takes, means the triumph of the flesh over the spirit. It means weakness and softness of character, and is the direct antithesis of that spiritual strength and virility which accompanies will-power. To give way habitually to sensuality means the abandonment of self-control and the death of the will. It means that concupiscence usurps the throne of the will; that sense and not the soul is master.

Of the more common form of sensuality, to which the wide term immorality is often restricted, M. Jules Payot well describes the consequences.[1]

"The health is seriously impaired by such

[1] "The Education of the Will" (English Transl.), p. 311.

excesses; the young people who commit them get an oldish look. They have a feeling of weakness in the back, muscular debility, and a sensation of pressure in the spinal cord, slight symptoms which pass unnoticed in the excitement of physical, animal exuberance. They lose their colour and freshness, their eyes look dull and heavy, and have dark rings under them. Their faces have a depressed look. Everything indicates a fatigue which, if frequently experienced, soon saps the very springs of life; it, to a certain extent, prepares the way for gastralgias, neuralgias, hypertrophy of the heart, and weakness of sight, all of which begin at about thirty years of age to make life miserable for those who have not been keen enough to foresee the consequences of indulgence. But the body is not the only thing to feel the disastrous influence of sensuality, the memory becomes astonishingly weak, and the mind loses all its buoyancy and vigour. It begins to feel dull and to move sluggishly, as if overcome by torpor. The attention is weak and wandering. The days slip by in apathetic indifference, accompanied by a feeling of listlessness and disheartening laziness. Above all there is that loss of virile joy in work, and it becomes a bore the moment it lacks its material recompense.

196

"Finally the habit of physical pleasure substitutes coarser and more violent emotions for the gentler but more lasting emotions of the mind. Their excitement and agitation destroy the joy that is to be found in calmer pleasures. And as sensual pleasures are short in duration, and are followed by fatigue and disgust, the character becomes habitually despondent and morose, with a sense of depression which drives one to find relief in violent, boisterous, brutal pleasures. It is a discouraging vicious circle."

That this picture is not overdrawn we know only too well. Every great Catholic preacher has at one time or another to paint it. In his "Conférences de Notre-Dame" Lacordaire thus portrayed the victims of "the depraved sense." "Those men who in the flower of their age already exhibit the ravages of time; who, degenerate before having attained the full birth of their being, display a brow that is prematurely lined, eyes that are vague and sunken, lips that seem powerless to represent goodness—they drag on, under a sun hardly risen, a worn-out existence."

The havoc wrought in the soul of the debauché is still worse than that wrought in his body. Grace, which sanctifies and beautifies the soul, is driven out. Darkness and disease replace light and health. The noble impulses which urge a pure soul towards God, the source of all goodness, give way to base instincts prompting towards selfish and vain pleasure. Conscience too is blunted, and the sense of what is right and just is dulled. What Père Gillet calls a "ferocious egoism" leads step by step to the ruin of the fair temple of the Holy Spirit.

The social evil consequent on sensuality is likewise considerable. The selfishness of immorality is proverbial. Suffering is inflicted on others without hesitation. Many are robbed of their rights that the cravings of one man's passion may be satisfied. We cannot refrain from quoting a further passage from the "Conférences" in which Lacordaire shows what an "anti-social" crime sensuality is. "I maintain," he said, "that I have never encountered tenderness in a libertine. I have never met a loving spirit but in those who were either ignorant of evil or were struggling against it. Because, once habituated to violent emotions, how can the heart, that is so delicate a plant, that is nourished by the dew falling from heaven, that is swayed by the lightest breath, made happy for days by the remembrance of the spoken word, by the glance bestowed, by the encouragement given to it by the lips of a mother, or the hand-grasp of a friend; how shall that which is so calm a movement, that which, naturally, is almost insensible, because of its very sensibility, and its alarm lest one breath of love should break it, if God had made it less profound,—how, I say, can this heart oppose its gentle and frail joys to those coarse emotions of the depraved sense? The one is selfish, the other generous; the one lives for self, the other outside self; of these two tendencies one must prevail. If the depraved sense has its way, the heart decays little by little— it loses its capacity for simple joys, it tends no longer towards others, it finally pulsates only in relation to the course of the blood, and marks the hours of that shameless time, the flight of which is hastened by debauchery."

It is not necessary to dwell further on the evil consequences, whether personal or social, of sensuality. Our point of view is entirely practical, and our sole duty is to consider how far will-psychology can aid religion in its work of fortifying the souls of the young against evil. As we have pointed out before, religion by itself affords a most effective training ground for character. Religion can

199

and does supply means for safeguarding the young against sensuality. By the practice of religion in using the sacraments, in praying, in assisting at Mass, abundant grace is obtained for fighting evil instincts, and not a few Catholic youths in every country, and perhaps very many, for we cannot tell how many, pass through the fire unburned. Professor Förster, a non-Catholic, thus writes: "Religion is so fundamental and indispensable that without it the young, especially those of strong temperament, will strive in vain to live continently and—if we except a few rare cases—to banish and overcome violent temptations." In grace men find their chief ally. That fact is certain, though of course some non-Catholics deny it. However, it is no less true that human means can also help to prepare the young for the battle against sensuality, and among these means the training of the will takes a foremost place.

We must now refer briefly to that problem which confronts educationalists as to the best method of "educating to purity."[2] Very diverse views are held on this matter, nevertheless German and American writers, Catholic

[2] *Vide*, "Educating to Purity," by Fr. Gutterer, S. J., and Fr. Krus, S. J.

and non-Catholic, on the whole seem to favour
a methodical, though of course very prudent,
instruction in "moral hygiene." Such instruction must as far as possible have religion as its
mouthpiece, and it must aim at inculcating the
need of moral strength. For knowledge of
good and evil, unaccompanied by the power
and grace to choose good and avoid evil, is unquestionably a danger.

"Education to Purity" must of course be
adapted to the special circumstances of a country. If, as it seems in Germany, there is a
veritable anti-purity propaganda, no doubt a
more complete instruction is possible and is
called for. Such a state of things appears to
prevail, at least, in some parts of Germany.
I quote a passage from Professor Paulsen's
work already referred to: "It appears as if
all the devils were let loose at present to lay
waste the domain of German social life. There
is an organised traffic promoting horrible
crimes. Raving women proclaim in pamphlets
and novels 'the right to motherhood,' twaddling
poets preach to ripe youth the necessity and
the right to pursue the pleasures of which some
people seek to deprive them. The newspaper
world, theatres, novels, lectures by men and
women, would seem to force upon the public

as the foremost question, 'must not all obstacles to free sexual life be driven from the earth?' "

There is no doubt that in many cases "sex-education" is overdone. Some men have a morbid anxiety to treat the question on all possible occasions, and often with infinitesimal discretion. Fr. Van der Donckt in his book,[3] "Educating to Purity," refers to such folk. "A further special danger of corruption lies in the craze for sexual enlightenment which—as if the easily excited imagination of children still needs violent stimuli—consists in the most heedless exposition and description of the merely physiological side of sexual matters, whereas the material side ought to be kept in the background through the emphasising of the moral."

Professor Förster, while admitting the necessity of a certain judicious instruction, recommends as the best type of indirect enlightenment instruction on the building up of will-power. He himself when asked to give a conference to a school on the sex-problem chose as his subject: "The Gymnastics of the Will." In so doing he pointed out what appears a very good solution of this difficult problem. His solution

[3] p. 28.

appears to be this—in the course of a lecture on the need and importance of strength of will, and self-control, to point out in a prudent way the attacks which are delivered by passion against the dominion of the soul. The nature of these attacks may be described with some reference to physiology, but emphasis should be laid on the force and holiness of grace, coming from the use of the sacraments, whereby man remains lord of himself, and the image of God.

For Catholics, the confessional is naturally the place for more delicate and more detailed instruction. And it is certainly within the scope of Catholic teachers to urge their boys to seek, in Confession, whatever instruction may allay their doubts and troubles of mind. Instruction in the confessional also has the advantage of avoiding that chief difficulty which educationalists experience of speaking to an audience of several persons on such matters. For with such an audience it is inevitable that what may be good and salutary for some may be unwholesome for others.[4]

[4] We cannot refrain from quoting, at this point, from a paper read at the "International Congress of Moral Education," held at The Hague in 1912, by Mlle. E. Simon, on the question of training the will in childhood.

"L'enfant est porté par instinct vers tout ce qui flatte les

Instruction for Catholics will, of course, recommend as "special safeguards" against sinful forms of sensuality, (1) Frequent Communion, (2) Devotion to the Blessed Virgin, (3) Hard Work and Penance. It will inculcate the need of high ideals and self-sacrifice for fellow-men. It will insist on a "fight to the finish" in spite of falls and lapses, and will show, on sound bases of history and physiology, the possibility of chastity and its great physical, intellectual, and moral blessings. It will propose too the examples of heroic virtue to be found in great number among the Saints of the Church, and will record the wise sayings of

sens et les procédés de l'éducation en usage aujourd'hui ne tendent que trop à développer ce penchant.

"Cette mollesse dont on se méfie peu est cependant pleine de dangers: elle rend incapable de tout vertu, elle ouvre la porte à tous les vices, elle enlève toute énergie au caractère, elle empêche la formation de la volonté en laissant l'âme subir le joug du corps et ce corps lui-même est sans force et sans vigueur. C'est pourquoi, en vue de combattre le sensualisme, on doit entredire à l'enfant les aliments et les boissons qui n'ont d'autre but que de flatter le palais, ses vêtements seront modestes et peu luxueux; on évitera par là tout ce qui peut encourager la vanité et faire naître les idées de supériorité. . . . On endurcira le corps par l'usage de l'eau froide et des exercises qui développent les muscles. En fait d'amusement qu'on ne perd jamais de vue que les concerts en général, les sorties du carnival, les théâtres, les bals d'enfants, font une triste impression sur l'âme et amollissent la volonté."

good men. "I have never," wrote a Swedish professor, Dr. Ribbing, "in my twenty years' experience with young and old, come across a single one who declared self-mastery in sexual matters impossible, provided, of course, there be good will."

We have dwelt somewhat at length on this subject for the reason that the will is looked on as man's natural weapon against sensuality, and chastity is called "the triumph of the will." Why this is so we shall now proceed to show, although of course in this context we speak not of the will in its purely natural state, but of the will inspired and strengthened by grace.

From experience we know that *action* arouses our noblest instincts. In the examples of strenuous lives we find inspiration. In the prospects of future action we place our ideals. To act and to achieve calls out all that is best from within us. The energy that then awakens is our purest and noblest force. And if it is invoked to serve a good purpose, we at once leave the shadows of sense-life for fields of action.

Now the life of action is the life of the will. It is the will that provokes to action. In doing so it not only limits and opposes sensuality, but it banishes it for the moment. It means that the life of the spirit takes the place of the life of the senses. That virility reigns instead of softness and day-dreaming.

The will, according as it grows stronger and is capable of more frequent and more strenuous efforts, naturally limits and opposes sensuality more and more. It begins to make attacks on luxuries, even legitimate luxuries, and awakens a tendency towards a "hard" life. We begin to rid ourselves under its influence of what is unnecessary. Perhaps we give up smoking, drinking wine, and wearing luxurious clothing. We begin to arise earlier in the morning, and more punctually, and we feel the need for harder work and more strenuous exercise. Still the life of the will, inspired of course by religion, leads us further afield, and we strive to cultivate the higher virtues of manhood that mean self-perfection. Sins of the flesh are now particularly odious to us, for they are the very essence of that sensuality which we have conquered. Nobler and higher ideals fill our minds and perhaps, should the grace be given us, we become great forces for good.

The life of the will then means the death of sensuality. But this must be prepared for by constant will-exercises. "The will must be thoroughly trained for years, as there is no specific which can be prescribed at the moment of danger." [5] Nothing can take the place of methodical exercises. "Will-power is built up by a gradual process of practice on the smallest things and every act of self-conquest in one sphere of life makes the battle easier in all the other spheres." [6] These exercises, inspired as they will be in the minds of Catholics by religious motives, will inevitably lead to self-conquest if faithfully persisted in. They cannot be replaced by irregular and ill-organised incursions into other methods of penance or mortification. An occasional discipline, or day spent in wearing a hair-shirt, or a triduum of fasting and chains, will not suffice. *Will-exercises must be methodical and well-regulated as to degree and length, or else they are perhaps worse than useless.*

To sum up, then, our views on the problem of the conquest of sensuality. To us the solution seems to lie in a good method of will-training inspired by and supported by religion. No doubt prudent education in moral doctrines is absolutely essential also. But the main force

[5] Professor Paulsen.
[6] Professor Förster.

from within, which is to fight and win the battle against sensuality, is will-force, developed by methodical exercises, and inspired by religion.

SECTION XV
FURTHER FACTS ABOUT THE WILL

SECTION XV

In this section we propose to record some observations on will-phenomena which may be of interest, and perhaps of use to students of will-psychology. We shall give them without any effort at classification, or order, and without claiming for them any particular value, save what is derived from the fact that they are the outcome of an experience of some thousands of experiments on the will. Drawn as they are from introspections they are naturally tinged with subjectivity, but that, as we have already pointed out, does not deprive them of all value and trustworthiness.

.   .   .   .

(1) *The Will Within*

In making efforts we are intimately conscious that *now, somewhere within,* there is an active driving-force, tending outwards and onwards. "Something deep and strong and of worth." [1] It is "something I have, yet which is myself." "It is not thought nor emotion nor feeling. Will-movement is something distinct from thought or emotion. It is a tendency of the soul with a consciousness of tending, and a warmth and colour about it." My will is I, an "active I"—"not knowledge, nor image, nor feeling, nor sensation." It is "earnest," "arbitrary," "moral," "practical." "The will was certainly there working within," and "*it* was going to go through the task," and so I "felt inclined to look and tend straight outwards, forwards," amid its "undulations and heaves." There is something "inexorable," "powerful and supreme," "practical," and "earnest," some personal force "acting along the predetermined lines" of a resolution.

(2) *The Will* Elan

It is called up, yet it seems to spring up naturally, unprovoked, and it does so again and again as if by habit. From whence does it come? And what limit is there to the number of times it can come? This "deep spontane-

[1] Quotation marks indicate verbatim quotation from *introspections*.

ous will-movement," this "strong heave of the will," "tides over a strain," intensifying the will-act, as it repeats itself. It is calm, not excited, but tiring. It is an indeliberate "will to will."

(3) *Will-Feeling*

Accompanies "the consciousness of doing something in virtue of a law." It marks "the being (actively) in harmony with a law." It is "dull, mental, non-sensual, steady, cheerful; a distinct central feeling," "a sense of doing." It marks "action rather than submission." "Time goes quickly when the characteristic, manly, reassuring will-feeling is present." There is something fresh, and strange about it, as though the action it accompanies "willing one's will" were an unaccustomed act. It is a bracing and ennobling feeling, and seems to tone one up.

(4) *Feeling and Willing*

A sense of satisfaction is sometimes experienced when the will is making efforts which are causing intense physical pain. This shows the difference between feeling and will, and "the *'anti-ness'* between the will and the physi-

213

cal part." "I realised that there is an infinite difference between feeling pain and difficulty and giving in." "Every fresh arm-ache brought back the will to make another effort." "The will is in its own sphere; physical suffering is in another."

(5) *Will-Set*

The will somehow becomes focused. It takes up a position and seems to tend in a direction. "The will was quite fixed and settled." "The set of the will is recognisable. It is very intimate, interior, and spiritual. It means a kind of direction." A kind of will-tension is experienced, and "introduces a universal tension in the body." When a resolution has taken root, the will becomes possessed of a certain semi-physical attitude. "My will is set and my hands will have to stop up there." "I saw and knew that my will was 'taken' and was for my hands being up there. So I knew that they would stop up there." "The will is firmly set, hence the task will be accomplished." Quite akin to this will-set is the *intention* as it appears in consciousness. "The intention takes the form of a dull forward movement towards a vague, dark, dimly understood blotch which stands for the task.''

(6) *Will-Associations*

Just as one image tends to draw another image into the field of consciousness, so one will-phenomenon tends to call up another will-phenomenon. The word *will* itself ''has a curious attraction and awakens deep associations.'' It provokes the will-feeling and ''awakens deep emotions.'' ''The word *will* awakened deep and noble sentiments.'' It seems somehow to arouse the will-atmosphere of which we spoke. ''It has associations of a deep nature.'' It drives away ennui. ''When the will is present ennui is absent.'' It stirs up a sense of confidence and power and a ''sense of nobility, and manfulness, and dignity.'' ''Will-feeling was awakened by the sound and sight of the word *will.*''

(7) *My Will*

''My will seems a redundant phrase.'' Certainly *my will* is something which I can, so to speak, stand and watch as a thing apart, and yet in doing so I feel that I am watching myself at work. ''My will seems a strange

215

phrase." *Will is not something possessed, it is something lived.* "I will train my will"— means self-commanding and obeying self. "I saw the effect (in myself) of obedience to my will." "The force of will in subjecting to itself the hand came home to me—this braced up my will." "I felt that my will was well in hand." "I stood watching the power of my will." At times we clearly see how we will will, how we provoke, by means of our will, will acts. "The will did not allow the will to waver or falter for an instant."

(8) *Intensity of Willing*

To will with full intensity it is necessary to have a strong motive, a well-defined end in view, a well-focused voluntary attention, freshness of mind and body, and important issues at stake which are clearly understood (implying "a scale of values clearly and definitely known"), finally confidence of triumph. "The intensity of willing seems to be measured by the certainty of the task being completed." The intensifying of the will-act is partly deliberate, partly indeliberate, for as we have seen the *élans* by which it is intensified come sometimes spontaneously and sometimes at one's call. *By willing will we strengthen the will-act.*

The signs of a really intense will-act are mainly these. The feeling of willing is more noticeable and deeper. We feel more wholly associated with and identified with the act. All our powers seem to be united and directed without hitch in the direction of the end in view.

(9) *Strengthening Motives*

To produce a really intense will-act our motives must be strengthened. This happens if the motive remains *alive* at the focus of consciousness for a time, or by virtue of contrast with less worthy motives, or by being subsumed under some acceptable general law, or by caprice, or by some physical act which brings it more forcibly before consciousness. The last means of motive-strengthening is seen in the following quotation: "The task grew easier as I gazed at my hands and said to myself, 'I've only to keep them there, and that isn't hard.'" Or again, "The strengthening thought was, 'the hands will stop up there all right for five minutes, don't be afraid.'" A feeling of assured confidence tends to strengthen motives as well as will. "The task, of course, will be fulfilled, and it has got to be fulfilled." This feeling is a "certainty of mind that I should achieve the fulfilment of the task."

(10) *Pleasure of Willing*

We often feel willing "to be grand, and refreshing, and bracing," but there is further a distinct feeling of pleasure—"a strange quiet feeling of pleasure in exercising this faculty of the will, for such I took it to be." There is a sentiment of dignity and cheerfulness which elevates this pleasure, "a feeling of dignity and self-respect." "I felt the nobility of doing a will-task." "I felt it a manly, noble thing to exercise the will." "I experienced a sentiment of moral satisfaction," and "felt brave, strong, full of will-power and confident."

(11) *Reality of Willing*

"I assured myself repeatedly that the will really willed to keep the hands up there. That was the only thing of importance. If the will to keep the hands up there was true, real and sincere, the hands would, of course, stop up there." When, in willing, *you mean,* then you know you mean. A real resolution is registered internally and acts very effectively. Often we connect physical effort with willing. It is not *it* but is connected with *it*. Physical movements, i. e., external signs of willing, seem to help on willing. Slow movements seem to help to greater deliberation. But perfect willing ought to be independent of such aids. *Real willing is allied with thoughts rather than with physical action.* The semblance of willing (to frown and square the jaws and clasp the fists tightly, etc.) should not be taken for the reality. Physical tension is no more *will* than feeling or emotion. "Willing should be closely connected with the mind. It should be the faithful and precise fulfilling of the resolution —not more nor less."

(12) *Concern About the End*

During a will-task thought is constantly turning towards the end. Is it far off or near? Shall I be able to hold out? A yearning is experienced, a need or want to be at the end. "I felt at once the craving to be at No. 100." "I realised that the will is *a tendency which needs to be satisfied.*" I felt a "tension to get the thing done," and was conscious of "tending towards the end," and of "an effort to reach

the goal." This impatience to satisfy the
conative desire is not always present. "I was
not overanxious to finish but was quite satisfied to be performing the task." *This "con-
cern about the end" emphasises how much the
will has to do with the future.* "The future always enters into will-acts." "I realised how
much one controls and commands the future by
a resolution." The will is "a reign of purpose,
endeavour, and seriousness," for the reason
that it means the striving for a *bonum,* for
something which will compel and perfect us.

(13) *Physical Exercise and Will*

"Physical exercises seem to brace me up and
stir up true willing better in me than petty
exercises. Is this because I am something
more of an animal than a thinking being?"
The reason perhaps is that such exercises, by
improving the circulation of the blood, render
it more easy to will, while the external movements may, by resembling the external signs
of willing or by amplifying them, help on willing. "The physical exercises seem to fit in
well with will—to go well with willing." Still
when some small, unimportant task is given
one experiences the sense of willing and sees

that any task may become a will-task. "I realised that triviality has nothing to do with the question of willing," that physical "easiness or difficulty does not matter." What does matter is "to act along the lines of a resolution."

(14) *Willing "Non-Will"*

It seems impossible to produce by a will-act a state of complete inertia, listlessness and *non-will*. One can become somewhat like an inert log but still the will is not wholly inactive. The will-element can be "diminished" considerably by awakening "sleepiness, weariness, and depression," but *it is impossible to wholly banish will*. The sensations of heaviness, inertia, aimlessness and ennui may be clearly present, but such states do not and cannot allay the will.

When acting *against the grain* a worried, fretful, depressed feeling is experienced, and the will seems to come to a stop-still. But this is more apparent than real. The will is acting all the time, though perhaps subconsciously.

. . . .

Such observations as those which we have given will, we fear, prove uninteresting to most of our readers. They will seem far-fetched and

221

perhaps hardly intelligible. In many cases our phrases will seem words and nothing more. But for those who have patiently studied the ways and moods of the will and who have *grasped the fact that the will is a vital something working within,* different from all our other faculties, and more subtle and delicate in its movements than any of them, these descriptions and reflections will not be without value. At worst they will prove suggestive, and will afford matter for speculation.

EPILOGUE

THE FUTURE OF WILL PSYCHOLOGY

EPILOGUE

It is a difficult matter to foretell the part that a particular science is to play in life. And in the case of a psychology it is all the more difficult. This is partly due to the fact that the actual progress that such a science is making is hidden; it cannot easily be observed. It is quite another thing with regard to a physical science. The swift and sure advances of electricity and chemistry are visible to every eye. The rate at which they are progressing is startling. But it is not so with psychological sciences.

That psychology is progressing we have no doubt. The new pedagogy has unquestionably forged ahead and solved some minor problems. The art of training memory and imagination has been perfected, and very useful additions to our knowledge of the "mind of the child" have been won. In other directions too the work of modern psychology has been far from fruitless; criminology, the study of nervous and mental diseases, hysteria, suggestion, and hallucination, the "psychology of the crowd" and of peoples, graphology, together with the psychology of the senses and of mysticism— these and other fields of research have been tilled by psychologists with success. But the fact still remains that no progress in any measure as definite or as obvious as that of physics or chemistry has been made.

There is no doubt that modern life shows a knowledge of psychology which in many ways is remarkable. As a single instance of this we have the modern art of advertising. But it is by no means sure that this new art is due to "scientific" psychology, and is not the application of keen business intellects to the problem of how to attract attention. In other provinces of psychology much the same may be said. There are few changes introduced into the up-to-date schoolroom which "the man in the street" could not have hit upon. Nor is there much in what psychology says of "suggestion" and "hallucination" which an intelligent physician would not have thought of for himself. But no one would assert the same of the discoveries in the domains of physical sciences. These are far beyond the abilities of

226

the plain man, and it needed a Marconi to discover wireless telegraphy and an Edison to invent the phonograph.

From all this it must not be thought that
the work of psychologists is futile or super-
fluous. It is less "sensational," if you will,
than the work of great chemists, but it is none
the less important. It is their part to pursue
and extend the knowledge that the human mind
has of itself. To advance little by little the
frontier line which parts the known from the
unknown in the various regions of the mind,
and to analyse with infinite patience those apparently insignificant and minor phases of
mental activity which are just observable and
little more. They must be content too, in many
cases, with the rewards which a theoretic science can give, for often their researches into
the human mind are such as to have little significance for the practical world outside.
Knowledge of this kind cannot beautify a man-
sion or make a tramcar run more smoothly.
But nevertheless it tends to satisfy a need in
the soul of man, and help him in some small
way towards his self-perfection.

Modern psychology then renders our knowledge of the mind more clear, more complete,
and more precise, besides of course extending

it somewhat—and in this lies its *raison d'être*.

Having thus far treated of psychology in general, we must now turn to consider will-psychology.

Will-psychology has, perhaps more than any other department of psychology, a practical bearing. It studies the guiding force that shapes and directs our lives. It is the science of the concrete principle of human action. It aims at gaining a knowledge of that principle which will enable us to perfect it and so perfect ourselves. It is intimately concerned in many grave problems of ethics and religion. In its progress lies our hope of solving some of the many difficulties which cluster round "character-formation." And it is not too much to say, if we admit as most of us do that reform must commence at home, within ourselves, that the progress of will-psychology is likely indirectly, at least, to help in social reform. But more sure will be its influence in the sphere of education, should it advance to any considerable extent.

We come now to ask ourselves the straight question, *What future lies before will-psychology?* Is it likely that the hopes placed in it will be fulfilled? Is the day to come when a really efficient system of will-training will prevail? and when men will be as well equipped with regard to their wills as they are to-day with regard to their intellects? In fine, is it probable that some change for the better will be wrought among men by improved methods of will-culture?

Before attempting even a partial answer to these questions, we propose to point out a few of the likely, or at least possible developments of will-psychology.

First of all, it is fair to suppose that the methods and technique of will-psychology will improve a great deal. They have already improved much, as the researches undertaken at Würzburg, Louvain and elsewhere show. It is fair, too, to suppose that a great increase will take place in the number and variety of researches in this department of psychology. There is a certain natural interest in will-problems which is likely to ensure this, especially when greater facilities for such researches are to be had. These facilities will be insufficient until many laboratories are set up with the sole object of will-research, and until a central laboratory for the purpose of coördinating the results gained is established.

When a sufficient number of laboratories are

set up investigations will be carried into many untrodden or but half-trodden fields. The volitional phenomena of normal and abnormal types will be carefully studied; children and savages, old and young, mad and sane, criminals and guiltless, Mongol and Aryan, all will become in turn subjects of research, and no investigation, however laborious or however bizarre, will be shirked.

From the accumulated results of such researches, pursued in every direction with all the painstaking industry of modern scientists, what are we to hope for? To those who have faith in modern psychology it is not hard to believe that such researches will be pursued and that in an honest way. But what results are to be looked for?

It is best for us to answer this question in a moderate way, minimising rather than exaggerating. Well, then, among other things it is possible that these researches will find means of determining different types of will [1]—just as there are different types of memory,—and that they will point out good methods of training each special type of will. It is possible that fairly sound methods of diagnosing and

[1] We do not mean that any *specific* differences can be found among wills, but only *accidental* differences.

treating will-maladies will be determined. It is possible that ingenious tests (*though we are sure they will never be at all conclusive*) will be discovered for measuring the individual's will-power. It is possible, too, perhaps it is better to say just barely possible, that some light may be thrown on some phenomena which are spoken of at present as "telepathic," and that the conditions most favourable to the transmission of some kind of will-influence may be approximately determined. Something more may be found out about hypnotism, and the part played by the will in cases of insanity. There will doubtless be progress in many other directions of will-psychology as well, and much more accurate knowledge will be forthcoming about motives, conative impulses, choice, decision, the means of intensifying will-acts and of developing the latent resources of the will.

To return now to the questions—Is the day to come when a really efficient system of will-training will prevail? Is it probable that some change for the better will be wrought among men by improved methods of will-culture? On the whole it seems fairly reasonable to give an affirmative answer to these questions. Many men are seriously anxious to find a good system of will-training and there seems no intrinsic or indeed extrinsic repugnance in the possibility of discovering it. Many men too would be benefited, we venture to say morally as well as in other ways, by utilising, as many certainly will, such a system. Further, and on this point we wish to lay some stress, it is far from improbable that such a system, when adapted to the educational needs of the young, would do much good. Indeed, it seems to us not unlikely that a somewhat new orientation in education will be initiated, sooner or later, when a really efficient system of will-culture is forthcoming.

Hitherto, whether we like to admit it or not, education (I speak, of course, of secular education, for it is not true of religious education) has been too much concerned with the furnishing and developing of the intellect. Memory, imagination and reasoning-powers have monopolised too much the attention of teachers. "Our ordinary training," writes Professor Mathews,[2] "is a training in knowledge; what the world needs is a training in power. Knowledge by itself is of no more value than a corn-seed left to dry and rot till all its fructifying power is gone; the pursuit of knowledge for

[2] "The Principles of Intellectual Education," Cambridge Press, p. 128.

its own sake is selfishness—the most dangerous form of it because the most subtle." It would seem that there is within us, quite wrongly, an inborn prejudice in favour of mind-culture as distinct from will-culture. Yet when we reflect we cannot help recognising that a man whose mind alone is developed is less than half a man. "We should turn out our children knowing less but using well the less which they do know, so that it would be a vital whole with vital power of growth, not that agglomeration of dead knowledge of the past which is too often now regarded as the real aim of education." [3] Success in examinations is taken as proving competency for work of various kinds. And yet it is well known that what employers look for most is not mental culture but those fine qualities of character, energy, consistency, decision, and perseverance which are rather the outcome of will-culture. Beyond question a flexible and exact intellect is a magnificent possession, but without will-power and self-restraint it is of little utility.

The new orientation in education would conceivably take the form of courses, theoretic and practical, in will-education in schools. It seems far-fetched now-a-days to talk of will-education

[3] op. cit., p. 128.

in secondary schools and colleges, but perhaps it is not unlikely that it will come about. Our forefathers would have stood aghast at the idea of the introduction of gymnastics and Swedish drill into schools and convents, and yet such a thing has come to pass. They would have scoffed at the realisation of Plato's dreams. But they would have been wrong in so doing.

Apart, too, from schools and colleges, it does not seem improbable that many a "plain man" will be found well versed in the theories of will-psychology, and quite prepared to undertake suitable will-exercises for his own self-perfection. In saying this, we feel the ground more sure under our feet, for we know of a certain number of cases of men of quite different interests and pursuits, who have undertaken such exercises, and, as they affirm, not without fruit.

It must not, we repeat again, be thought that will-culture can ever replace in any way religion, or that will-culture of itself has an ethical significance, but nevertheless we cannot think of any kind of self-culture which harmonises so well with religion and with morality.

Should it ever happen, then, that will-culture was taken up widely and popularly—as,

of course, is not likely, but just possible—
we feel sure that "a change for the better"
would be wrought among men. There would be
less sensuality and less dishonesty among those
who thus strive to train their wills. It would
serve for them in some sense as "a new force"
and would inspire them to some high and noble
enterprises.

It is not unlikely that will-training would
have a beneficial effect in curing or partly curing many maladies of the nerves. Even mental diseases might thereby be banished. For,
as we have said more than once, will-power is
the greatest and purest natural force that we
are possessed of, and it is capable of achieving very great results. It does not seem too
much to say that some good might be wrought
in prisons, among criminals (among those
especially whose religion is a negligible quantity) by teaching them how to exercise their
powers of self-restraint, and how to control
their passions by the natural powers of the
mind. But, needless to say, in such cases almost the only hope lies in winning them to the
practice of religion.

Professor Jacks [4] has pushed some of these
thoughts too far, of course, but in an interest-

[4] "The Alchemy of Thought."

ing way when writing on the possibility of a *Science of Man*.

"That the intellectual temper of our time encourages the belief in the possibility of the Science of Man, and the hope of its realisation in the future, admits of little doubt. A state of the world when the system of natural laws shall be thoroughly understood, and when all human action shall be in accordance with this knowledge, is the far-off divine event to which vast numbers of persons are vaguely looking forward.

"This millennium of science has been often described. Physiology and its cognates shall enable us to control our bodies; we shall eat by science, dress, warm, and house ourselves by science. Psychology will have given us command of our minds; we shall know how our intellects, our emotions, our wills, act under given conditions, and we shall prepare them for acting accordingly; education will be thoroughly scientific; we shall teach nothing but what the laws of the mind allow the young to assimilate, and to assimilate in the most favourable manner."

This millennium, of course, never will come. Nor will a millennium of will-culture come. But there seems reason to hope that the future of will-psychology, as regards its practical results, will neither be uneventful nor barren. To us, this science seems the noblest of natural sciences, yielding place not even to medicine, for it aims at discovering the laws whereby man may be put more and more in possession of that supreme and kingly force which lies within him and which we name, *Strength of Will.*

APPENDIX

THE SCIENCE OF CHARACTER

APPENDIX

THE SCIENCE OF CHARACTER

It is generally admitted that in recent years experimental psychology has made remarkable advances. These advances consist mainly in the acquisition of a more exact knowledge of the nature of various mental activities— and, in some cases, in the discovery of certain minor, but none the less interesting phases of the functioning of the mind. Such advances are due almost wholly to the perfecting of the methods of the science, and to the extraordinary industry and perseverance of modern experimental psychologists.

It seems hardly necessary to revert to the oft-explained distinction between rational and experimental psychology, and yet there continues to be so much misunderstanding of the point that it is essential to do so. Briefly, then, the former science, the old-time rational, metaphysical psychology, treats of the *nature* or *essence* of the soul. It proves the soul to be

241

simple, substantial, spiritual, immortal. Its proofs are rigid, and in a legitimate sense it is a complete or finished science. It "holds the truth," and its duty is now to teach the truth, to "define it well."

Quite distinct from this is experimental psychology. It is a natural science of the mind. It observes, experiments, as far as it is possible to experiment on the mind, or will; it amasses and classifies phenomena and facts; it expands and advances with every new discovery. It does not enquire into the *nature* or *essence* of the soul, but it describes and analyses the activities of the soul. It is, in fine, a kind of chemistry or physics of the mind, in so far as there can be a chemistry or a physics of a spiritual substance.

Now the facts acquired by this natural science are, so to speak, handed on to the rational psychologist, and he builds his argument on these empirical data. He relies on the principle of St. Thomas, *actio sequitur esse*. And thus, "starting from the knowledge acquired in empirical psychology regarding the character of the operations and activities of the mind, he draws further conclusions as to the root or subject of those activities."[1]

[1] Father Maher, "Psychology," p. 6.

The advances made by experimental psychology, to which I have referred, led many to hope that in the domain of the science of character the new methods would also win great discoveries. Some went so far as to hope that a means would be devised for reducing character to a *formula*. Should this hope ever be realised, it would happen that applicants for places or positions, instead of presenting letters of recommendation, would draw forth from their pocket-books certificates signed by expert psychologists, containing their precise character-formula. That such a dream should be ever realised is most unlikely. "The globe," writes a Scotch essayist,[2] "has been circumnavigated, but no man ever yet has; you may survey a kingdom and note the result in maps, but all the savants in the world could not produce a reliable map of the poorest human personality." Character never will and never can be fully known. Such is the conclusion which forces itself upon every reasonable man, when he considers the extraordinary complexity of human character. Still, a certain judicious approximation can be made. Character can be *read* to some extent. It can even, to some extent, be reduced to formula. This for-

[2] Alexander Smith.

mula will approach nearer and nearer to the truth with the perfecting of experimental psychology. It is of this gradual advance of the science of character that I intend to write in this section.

We now must turn to the question of *character*—and begin by asking ourselves, what it is. First of all, it is the external clothing of *personality*—it is found only in the rational, individual nature, in the moral being. It is something liable to change and to modification, whereas *personality* remains unchanging and unchangeable. It is, then, something more on the surface, external, ephemeral, insubstantial, while lying, nevertheless, deep-founded in our mystic nature. Its elements are, on the one hand, constant, springing from an immutable nature; and on the other hand, inconstant, springing from casual circumstances. It is "the total collection of man's acquired moral habits grafted into his natural temperament." [3] Partly inherited and founded in the frame given us by our parents; partly formed by deliberate and partly by indeliberate personal activities; partly something inscrutable, *insaisissable,* completely spontaneous, defying both analysis and definition, it is an amal-

[3] Maher, "Psychology," p. 391.

gam of nature's and nurture's gifts—unified, blended, inspired.

Character has a manifold complexity of its own, and there seem to be difficulties utterly insurmountable in the way of an exact knowledge of it. First of all, there is the presence of that quality in the will which gives us an almost divine power, the quality of freedom. As free beings we can say *"No!"* even to God. This supremely spiritual endowment, defying all analysis, eluding all exact knowledge, is the central quality of character. By it a man who has a million times acted in a definite, characteristic manner when a certain occasion presents itself, may possibly, and certainly has the power to, act differently when the million and first occasion presents itself. Again, there is an extraordinary *resourcefulness* in every spiritual being. Who can gauge the possibilities that lie hidden beneath even the meanest human nature? The greatest and most confirmed cowards have on occasions surprised all the world by acts of bravery. Men of colossal stupidity have at times acted with supreme skill and tact. Indecision and hesitation, that seemed invincible, have given place to energy and resoluteness. In fine, as long as the body keeps within it a soul, it possesses a source of activity that may reveal itself in the least expected ways.

The vagueness of the descriptions or definitions of character, even by the most brilliant writers, strikes every careful reader. As an example let us take Lacordaire's description: "L'énergie sourde et constante de la volonté, je ne sais quoi d'inébranlable encore dans la fidélité à soi-même, à ses convictions, à ses amitiés, à ses vertus, une force intime qui jaillit de la personne et qui inspire à tous cette certitude que nous appelons la sécurité." What is the "force intime" to which Lacordaire refers? What is the "énergie sourde et constante" of the will? Doubtless he refers to that *possibility within us of making efforts,* of whatever kind these efforts may be. Since the point is important it seems worth while to venture on an analysis of "effort."

Let us again suppose ourselves on a cold day, at the end of a spring-board, about to take a plunge, but still hesitating. What are the elements of our total field of consciousness? (1) We know we have the power to make the effort, *to take possession of our wills* and so to set the human machine in motion. (2) We know that certain immediately painful and ultimately agreeable sensations will ensue. (3) We are conscious of a feeling of hesitation, instability, and uncertainty, and of a distinct nerve-strain. (4) Our attention is at once focused and distracted. Many unimportant details catch our attention, such as the frayed edge of the spring-board carpet—and yet such details do not distract our minds from the central focus, the thought of the plunge. (5) Then we have a feeling of doom, the dreadful choice-doom; for one or other alternative must be embraced. (6) Next, there is the surge and ebb of various minor impulses. "Come! *now!* he's looking at me! *No!* not yet! wait a second! the sun is coming out!" (7) Then the idea-image of oneself swimming gaily about, or some other idea-image begins to develop, and the muscles begin to adjust themselves. (8) A desire to act grows on us, the sense of losing consciousness of what is happening comes upon us; and (9) with a certain half-conscious, half-unconscious *fiat* we plunge in. The last stage of all is either too simple or too complex to be exactly described. Up to the last we feel we have power to linger on the board or to spring in, and now! we find ourselves in the water.

This analysis [4] of what is commonly called

[4] Experimental analyses of volitions cannot in themselves prove the freedom of the will; but on the other hand systematic

"effort," shows how real is that "force in-time" referred to by Lacordaire. It is the source of our "efforts," that is, the source of our most important power. It is the supreme quality of strong characters to be able to make and reiterate efforts. On this quality their genius, as well as their strength and consistency, depends. In the words of a Belgian metaphysician, "Le génie, c'est l'obstination" (Genius is obstinacy).

We have seen, then, how complex character is. Its resourcefulness, relativity, constancy mingled with inconstancy, together with the fact of freedom, and its central spontaneous power of making efforts, seem to force on us, at once, the conclusion "that it is impossible to determine character-formulæ, and that any attempt to do so would be absurd." We can know but few of the forces acting on the individual, we can know but little of his power to resist such forces, and yet did we know both the one and the other, we should still, on account of his freedom, be unable to prophesy definitely what action would result from the play of those forces.

Though it seems, then, so difficult, nay, so

experimental analyses of volitions go to show the utter worthlessness of the psychological arguments of Determinists.

impossible, to determine in exact terms a given character, still it must be admitted that humanity persists in the belief in the possibility of an accurate and precise reading of character. Business men stake fortunes on ventures which depend on the habits and idiosyncrasies of individuals. Nations trust their welfare to the integrity and honour of single statesmen. The united representatives and princes of the Church place the happiness and the welfare of the faithful in their reading of the character of some poor priest whom they choose as Pope. Saints and leaders accept or reject the services or companionship of postulants on their swift personal discrimination of their characters.[5] Nothing is so common in ordinary life as prophesyings about the future of "so-and-so"—"he will end his days on the gallows," "he will do great things for his country." Then comes the inevitable shaking of the head, and the "I told you so." Again, have not we ourselves our *moods*—our character categories —which are well known to our friends? Such things make us sulk, such things make us gay, such things amuse, or weary, or worry us. The

---

[5] Business men and others do not prescind from free will in forming estimates of characters—for they are the first to *blame,* to *praise* and to hold each one *responsible* for his actions.

little cycle of moods passes, and once more we sulk again. Those who have to deal with boys know how easy it is often to tell, almost to the minute, how long the boy's mood will last.

Then, a strange thing when we think of it, the more perfect the character is, the easier it is to prophesy concerning it. Friends of St. Dominic, or St. Francis, or St. Ignatius could tell almost with certainty what their views would be, or what attitude they would adopt in view of certain circumstances. They were men of rigid noble principles—and their will clung strongly to those principles—and their freedom was, thanks to their virtues, a free choice of the best, the *summum bonum*. Or, if we take the characters of O'Connell, Lincoln, Washington, Pitt—in each case there was a striking continuity, each case presented great traits which were followed throughout life. This need of consistency of action is founded, as we have seen, in our very nature. It means economy of energy, of will-force. It means that we have habits—and that we act and choose according to definite lines—and that our motives follow certain tracks.[6] George Eliot, in

[6] *Vide*, "Motive Force and Motivation Tracks," Longmans, 1911.

"The Mill on the Floss,"[7] describing the lawyer, Wakem, wrote:—"Mrs. Tulliver had suggested to him several determining motives and his mental glance was very rapid; he was one of those men who can be prompt, without being rash, because *their motives run in fixed tracks* and they have no need to reconcile conflicting aims."

The existence, then, of habits, consistency, and continuity of character, hereditary and acquired tendencies, together with all those forces which unite to make man, in a certain way, an automaton, as well as the existence of those immaterial motivation tracks, elsewhere described, result in justifying the pretensions of those who seek to read characters, and who seek to determine formulæ of characters. Once more we repeat that a perfect formula is impossible. Man is free to the last to break through his habits, to falsify his formula. But in his normal state he lives according to his formula—in his normal everyday life he lives through his cycle of moods and categories—and is known as "old so-and-so" by his friends. But how is "old so-and-so" to be examined scientifically and microscopically, so as to have his formula determined? For that we must

[7] Chap. vii.

turn once more to experimental psychology—
or rather to that volitional act, the choice-act,
which it is most competent to analyse.

The choice-act is the most wonderful act of
which we are capable. It is our most spiritual,
our most complex, and our most intimate personal act. It springs, so to speak, from the
central fountain of our soul. It is vital, immanent, intensely personal. It may be brief,
and pass almost unnoticed, but it is, nevertheless, the one act which betrays what we are,
and what we are capable of. It displays
abroad what is inmost in us. In the choice we
make, in our manner of choosing, in our hesitations, impulses, hedonic attractions and repulsions, in our firmness or weakness in embracing the favoured alternative, we reveal ourselves. As we dwell apart in that strange
sphere of choice—held captive between the
two alternatives A and B; now tending towards
one, now towards the other; suitors and foes in
turn; tossed hither and thither by the winds
of fancy; we feel, often, oppressed, humiliated,
and deceived, and we cry out our secrets. The
choice-act is, then, above all acts, that in which
our *character* is revealed. For Ruskin, to
study a man's *likes* was to study his character.
Certainly to study his likes and *how* he likes

is to study his character. To do so is to study his choice-acts, and in them, it is not too much to assume, all the essential elements of his character are revealed.

"In the choice-process a man reveals himself completely. Choice implies acting on *motives,* and nothing gives a deeper insight into man's nature than the knowledge of his motives, for they show us whether sense of duty or hedonic attraction plays the chief part in his life. Again, to choose is to put oneself in motion, to act; not necessarily to act exteriorly, but to act, at least, within. But action at once betrays the strength or weakness, the resoluteness or indecision of him who acts. Choice, too, implies motivation, and in motivation our power of reasoning (of insight into things), of calm and tranquil thought, is shown. In motivation impulsiveness, caprice, inconsistency, and carelessness, or the opposite qualities, are inevitably manifested." [8]

Seeing, then, that character is primarily revealed in the choice-act, the method for studying character must be substantially that for studying choices. The choice-act must be submitted to a close and searching analysis. Elements of character must be drawn apart, clas-

[8] "Motive Force and Motivation Tracks," pp. 205, 206.

sified, and observed in every way, and experimented on as far as possible. To do so, however, is essentially difficult. The only way we have of knowing what kind the choice was in itself is by the introspection of the chooser; and introspection, though a sound and useful method, is by no means a perfectly satisfactory method.

Being condemned to the use of this one instrument—introspection—in our study of the choice-acts of an individual, with the ultimate end of determining his character-formula, we arrange and devise a numerous series of simple choices, to be made under optimal conditions for introspective observation. Every facility is afforded the chooser for observing what passes within him and for having it recorded in writing.

It may be well, here, to give a brief account of the method employed by the present writer, in a series of experiments on the will and character conducted at Louvain University. It is typical of the experimental methods of those who are in sympathy with the Würzburg School of Psychology, a school which is distinctly Scholastic in its reliance on and reverence for *introspection*.

The subjects learned by heart eight differently-flavoured liquids, to each of which a non-sense-name was attached. The liquids were colourless, and indistinguishable, save by their tastes. The subjects, when they had come to know them by their names, and had proved that knowledge by *Recognition* experiments, drew up *Scales of Value,* placing the liquids in order of agreeableness and the reverse. Some liquids were very agreeable, some very unpleasant. Choice experiments now began. The nonsense-names, taken in pairs, were printed on cards and presented to the subjects by Ach's card-changing machine. Under the card were placed the two classes referred to by the names on the card. The subjects were *instructed* as follows: "Two words will appear simultaneously corresponding to the substances which are contained in the two glasses. You are to make your choice between these substances, and to drink at once the liquid which you have chosen."

The time of the choice, from the appearance of the card to the re-action (given by raising the finger to take a glass and drink) was measured by the Hipp chronoscope to the thousandth of a second. The subject was required, immediately after each experiment, to give an exact account of all that passed through his mind. These introspections were afterwards analysed and compared with great care.[9]

By means of this method, when a subject had made a few hundred choices, his intellectual and volitional nature was, to a great extent, revealed. All his hedonic tendencies, their frequency, and their force; all his hesitations and oscillations, were numbered, classified and measured. Efforts made to overcome hesitation, and immediate effects of hesitation; discouragement, irritation, inconsistency, etc., were all noted and examined. Again, impulsive tendencies, capricious movements, evidences of higher or lower motives, rhythmic motions to and fro between alternatives, or rhythmic turnings from one motive to another; in fine, every type of psychological phenomenon bearing on choice was analysed. If a subject chose for intrinsic motives and strengthened his motives by an appeal to some higher principle or axiom; and if his choices became smoother, easier, more regular, swift and automatic, it was clear that his will was functioning well, and that will-power was being economised. On the other hand, if a subject chose for extrinsic motives, if he only strength-

[9] For further account of the method see "Motive Force and Motivation Tracks."

ened such motives by an appeal to some purely
accidental circumstance, in fine, if he fell into
long and painful hesitations, and into inconsistencies, and if his choices, instead of growing smooth and automatic, grew jerky, unpleasant, and irregular, it was clear that his
will was functioning badly, and that will-force
was being wasted.

Again, if, when compared with other subjects, his motives proved more hedonic, his hesitations more frequent and more violent, his capricious acts more numerous (or, if the contrary was the case), a new insight into his character was gained. By comparison with other
subjects many interesting points could be determined. And by comparison with an *ideal
type,* formed by taking the mean, with respect
to important elements of character, in the cases
of several subjects, much could be gained.
Such an *ideal type* might thus be formed. If,
say, ten subjects, having gone through a certain number of similar experiments, of the type
just described, showed signs of hesitation in,
say, 5, 6, 15, 25, etc., per cent. of their choices,
the *ideal type* might be supposed to hesitate
in the percentage which represented the mean
of 5, 6, 15, 25, etc.

Such a method of forming an *ideal type* of

character is obviously open to many objections. "Hesitation," "hedonism," "capriciousness," are not things to be numbered or measured or weighed. Character is not like a plumpudding, composed of so many ingredients, taken in so many quantities. It is too vital and complex and spiritual to be thus treated. Our only plea for a hearing is that we are striving, though lamely of course, to suggest a concrete, practical method of determining approximate character-formulæ.

When, at length, we have determined the proportionate amount of hedonism, indecision, inconsistency, etc., in the character we are studying, it only remains, in order that we may write his character in the form of a formula, to determine on symbols. In the work on Will Psychology, already quoted, the following formula is given for S^2 (one of the subjects of the series of experiments).

$$S^2 = \text{Act. } 1\cdot5 + \text{Res. } 1 + \text{Hed. } 3 + \text{Hes. } 2 + \text{Incon. } 2\cdot5 + \text{Aesth. } 1 + \text{Repr. } 0\cdot5 \ldots \text{[10]}$$

[10] *Act.*=Active Tendencies, *Res.*=Resistance to Tendencies, *Hed.*=Hedonism, *Hes.*=Hesitation, *Incon.*=Inconsistency, *Aesth.*=Aestheticism, *Repr.*=Representations, Images, etc. This formula could, with further research, be rendered much more complete. Such items as *Incon.*, *Res.*, etc., are capable of analysis and breaking up into many further qualities.

258

We have, here, put intellectual and conative phenomena side by side. We have been at a loss to determine what the chief element of character is. Our proceeding is *simply and purely empirical.* We state that, *de facto,* under the conditions of our experiments, the formula given above approximately represents the intellectual and volitional nature of S^2, as compared with the standard described above. We are aware that the formula is incomplete and open to criticism. We merely propose it as a tentative effort.[11]

The obvious objection against any attempt of this kind to reduce something so vital, so many-sided, so dynamic as character to a formula, is that no percentage or quantitative expression of volitional and intellectual phenomena comes near to representing it. It is something deeper, something more immanent, something more "insaisissable."

We have stated that character reveals itself in the choice-act, and that the choice-act is the most important act that we perform. It follows, then, that especial care should be devoted to our method of choosing. Some choices are well made, others very badly made. Some choices are firm, calm, and certain, agreeable

[11] op. cit., p. 213.

in feeling tone, even and smooth in "movement." Other choices are feeble, uncertain, uneven and painful; far from bracing us up, as so important a mental act should, they leave us debilitated. To choose well should, then, be our aim, in view of training and developing our character, and to teach others to choose well is to show them how to perfect their character. To acquire a habit of choosing for good motives, in a deliberate, confident manner, is to improve immensely our character—indeed, it may be admitted that the psychology of motivation and the psychology of character are practically identical.

What, it may be asked, is the secret of choosing well, and in consequence of perfecting character? The answer would seem to be that *normally,* at least, the secret of choosing well is to form an accurate and clear estimate of the values of the alternatives between which we choose. "The central fact of the researches we have been describing is that, when a choice has to be made between two alternatives, the choice is quick and easy, in proportion as the values of the alternatives are *clearly and definitely* known." [12] We must, then, clearly and definitely determine the values of alternatives,

[12] cf. above, pp. 78-79.

260

and that, of course, if possible, long before the choice begins. We must have our fixed scale of values. We must have a scale of values for every sphere in which we live, and for our life as a whole. There must be a top-value, a *ne plus ultra* with which nothing whatever is comparable for us. It must be the top-value of St. Paul or St. Ignatius, if we would reach their extraordinary strength of purpose and noble consistency.

Then, again, there must be a lowest, a bottom-value, something which must never be chosen. There must also be middle-values and perhaps neutral-values. Into such details it is not necessary to enter. The main fact (as shown by the researches to which I have referred) must be kept in mind if we would learn the secret of choosing well, and so perfecting our character. It is, that our scale of values must be clearly and definitely known—each grade rigidly fixed and partitioned off from that above, and from that below.

To such a solution of the problem of how to choose well, the obvious objection is that at times we know and see clearly that one thing is more valuable than another, yet we take what is worst: *video meliora proboque, deteriora sequor*. Something, then, further than the mere clear and definite knowledge of a scale of values is required? To answer this objection we may point out that what we are seeking to give is the *practical* solution of the problem.

We do not, of course, deny that it often happens that one course is clearly and definitely known to be better than another, and yet that the other is followed. Still we believe that such a case is less frequent. The more frequent antecedent of wrong conduct is a *confused,* uncertain state of mind.

We have seen, so far, that thanks to Will Psychology, which enables us to analyse choices in a methodical way, we are in a position, in certain circumstances, to determine the character-formulæ of individuals. We have seen, too, that the perfecting of character is nothing else than the perfecting of our choice-powers; and that whereas personality is, and will remain, a riddle, and separate individuals will ever be to each other as Border peel is to Border peel on Tweedside, nevertheless, for practical purposes, character may be sufficiently discovered and made known. Indeed, the supposed impenetrability of character would seem to be frequently exaggerated by authors for literary effect:—

"A person [writes Smith] interests or piques or tantalises you. You do your best to make him out, yet strive as you will, you cannot read the riddle of his personality. From the invulnerable fortress of his own nature he smiles contemptuously on the beleaguering armies of your curiosity and analysis."

This, indeed, is hardly true, and the task set before the psychologist of character is neither so hopeless nor so difficult.